30-SECOND
ECONOMICS

30-SECOND
ECONOMICS

The 50 most thought-provoking
economic theories, each explained
in half a minute

Editor
Donald Marron

Contributors
Adam Fishwick
Christakis Georgiou
Katie Huston
Aurélie Maréchal

ICON

First published in the UK in 2011 by
Icon Books Ltd
Omnibus Business Centre
39–41 North Road, London N7 9DP
email: info@iconbooks.net
www.iconbooks.net

This book was conceived,
designed and produced by
Ivy Press
210 High Street, Lewes
East Sussex, BN7 2NS, UK
www.ivypress.co.uk

Creative Director Peter Bridgewater
Publisher Jason Hook
Editorial Director Caroline Earle
Art Director Michael Whitehead
Designer Ginny Zeal
Illustrator Ivan Hissey
Glossaries & Profiles Text Nic Compton
Picture Research Katie Greenwood

ISBN: 978-1-84831-232-6

Printed and bound in China

Colour origination by
Ivy Press Reprographics

10 9 8 7 6

CONTENTS

INTRODUCTION
Donald Marron

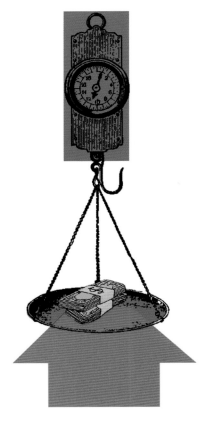

Economics wants to be the physics of the social sciences. Physicists examine how fundamental natural forces shape everything from the movements of subatomic particles to the orbits of heavenly bodies. Economists, in turn, study how fundamental social forces explain everything from the price of bread to the wealth disparity between the United States and Zimbabwe.

The theme of this book is that economists have been succeeding, but economics will never be physics. Over the past two centuries, economists have developed a host of theories – many described in the pages that follow – that explain how markets work and sometimes fail, how consumers, workers, firms and politicians make decisions, and why economies grow or stagnate.

Those theories have their limitations, however, because humans are less predictable than particles and planets. Economies are complex (more like ecosystems) and so our understanding of them sometimes falls short; our near-universal failure to foresee the worst financial and economic crisis in eight decades is a sorry but perfect case in point.

The science of economics is thus still a work in progress; and it may end up resembling biology more than it does physics. But economics isn't just a science. Many economists, myself included, believe that our insights into how the world works have implications for how the world should work in general. As a result, the scientific theories of economics blur into political theories of the good society.

Both sets of theories – the scientific and the political – can have great impact. As John Maynard Keynes once put it: 'The ideas of economists and political philosophers, both when they are right and when they are wrong, are more powerful than commonly understood. Indeed, the world is ruled by little else. Practical men, who believe themselves to be quite exempt from any intellectual influence, are usually the slaves of some defunct economist.'

Many of the top fifty theories in economics can indeed be traced to economists who are defunct, at least in the biological sense (including Keynes himself). But the theories themselves remain vibrant. As Keynes warns, however, important theories are not always right. So mixed among the most important theories you will find a few that are almost certainly wrong, despite their influence. See if you can find them.

Each 30-second theory is presented alongside a 3-second crash for those in a particular hurry, in addition there is a 3-minute boom for those who want to delve a little deeper. The first group of economic theories, **Schools of Thought**, examines the large-scale forces – markets, inertia, history – that determine how the macroeconomy actually works. **Economic Systems** then presents theories of how economies should be structured – with greater and lesser faith in markets – and how struggling economies can improve. In **Economic Cycles**, we look at the factors that drive economic ups and downs and the possible role of government in smoothing them. **Growth** examines how the proper blend of capital, labour, resources, ideas and social institutions can foster prosperity. **Global Trade** looks internationally, explaining how products and capital flow around the world. **Choice** peers into our heads in order to see how individuals make decisions in the marketplace, in the home, and in the public sphere. **Tax & Spend Policies** examines the sometimes surprising effects of government tax and spending policies. **Markets**, finally, documents the remarkable power of market forces, from the miracle of the invisible hand to the tragedy of the commons. Along the way, each section presents a quick profile of some of the most important economists, from Adam Smith to John Maynard Keynes to Milton Friedman.

How should you enjoy this book? Well, the individual essays are great for sampling but, as with potato crisps, you probably won't be able to stop with just one theory. Enjoy.

SCHOOLS OF THOUGHT

SCHOOLS OF THOUGHT
GLOSSARY

aggregate demand The total demand for goods and services within an economy at a certain time. This can be influenced by government either through monetary policy (that is controlling the amount of money in the economy) and/or fiscal policy (that is increasing/decreasing the amount of government expenditure).

exchange value The theoretical value for which a product or service can be traded – as opposed to the actual value for which it is traded, which is its price. Exchange value can be described as the *quantitative* value of a commodity, as opposed to use value, which is its *qualitative* value.

fiscal policy The way in which government uses public spending and taxation to influence a country's economic performance. Thus, a government may choose to tax more and invest in social security and public works, such as roads and hospitals, to create employment, and to increase salaries. Or it may choose to reduce public spending in order to reduce taxation, so that people have more money to spend in the first place. It's swings and roundabouts!

Keynesianism A school of thought created by the British economist John Maynard Keynes in the 1930s. Unlike most economists of the day, who believed that the market mechanism produces the most efficient outcome, Keynes believed that the market needed to be tempered by government intervention. He advocated the use of countercyclical fiscal policies, whereby the government pumps money into the economy when times are hard, but reduces spending when times are good.

laissez-faire An economic approach that advocates minimum government intervention (from the French, meaning 'let it be'). Proponents of this approach believe that the market will achieve the most efficient outcome and that government regulations distort the reality of the market, leading to inefficiency.

monetary policy The way in which government uses the supply of money – or, more specifically, interest rates – to influence a country's economic performance. Generally, low interest rates tend to increase the amount of money in circulation, which can help stimulate an economy during a recession; high interest rates tend to reduce the supply of money and can be used to reduce inflation.

rational expectations The assumption, used in many economic models, that people or companies make decisions by rationally evaluating the likelihood of possible future outcomes and the benefits or costs of those outcomes. This theory is useful, but can be misleading since people are not always rational or forward-looking when they make decisions.

stimulus policy The use of government policy to reinvigorate a flagging economy. This typically takes the form of spending on public works and/or tax breaks. Critics argue that this distorts the market and disadvantages private enterprise.

supply and demand This is the fundamental model of a market economy. It stipulates that the greater the demand for a product, the higher its price will be, until supply outstrips demand. At this point, the price will fall until an equilibrium is achieved between quantity and price.

use value The utility of a commodity within society. This is measured by the need or desire for that object. A classic example is a diamond, which, as an object, is of little real use, and yet its use value in most modern societies is nevertheless very high. Use value can be described as the *qualitative* value of a commodity, as opposed to exchange value, which is its *quantitative* value.

CLASSICAL
the 30-second theory

Writing in the eighteenth century, Adam Smith argued that the natural functioning of the market would always ensure stability and prosperity. For Smith, the market provided a site for the fulfilment of the natural human tendency to 'truck, barter and trade', while the market's 'invisible hand' reconciled these individual activities to maintain an equilibrium. In bringing together all the transactions made by individuals, the market also brings together their rational responses to moments of crisis. In essence, the market responds rapidly to any shocks without the need for state intervention. Government stimulus policies only restrict the market's ability to form a new equilibrium: they artificially boost incomes at times of crisis, temporarily supporting an increasingly unstable equilibrium. Such policies come at great expense to the taxpayer, and only store up problems for the future. Robert Lucas Jr recently extended such insights in regard to the impact of economic policy. He argues that the 'rational expectations' of individuals towards a specific policy will affect the way they react and so determine the impact of the policy itself. Policy cannot fool individuals into particular responses. Instead, only if the credibility of government is sufficient can policy modify individuals' behaviour against that brought about by market adjustment.

3-SECOND BIOGRAPHIES
ADAM SMITH
1723–1790

ROBERT LUCAS JR
1937–

30-SECOND TEXT
Adam Fishwick

'In the midst of all the exactions of government, capital has been silently and gradually accumulated by the private frugality and good conduct of individuals, by their universal, continual, and uninterrupted effort to better their own condition.'
ADAM SMITH

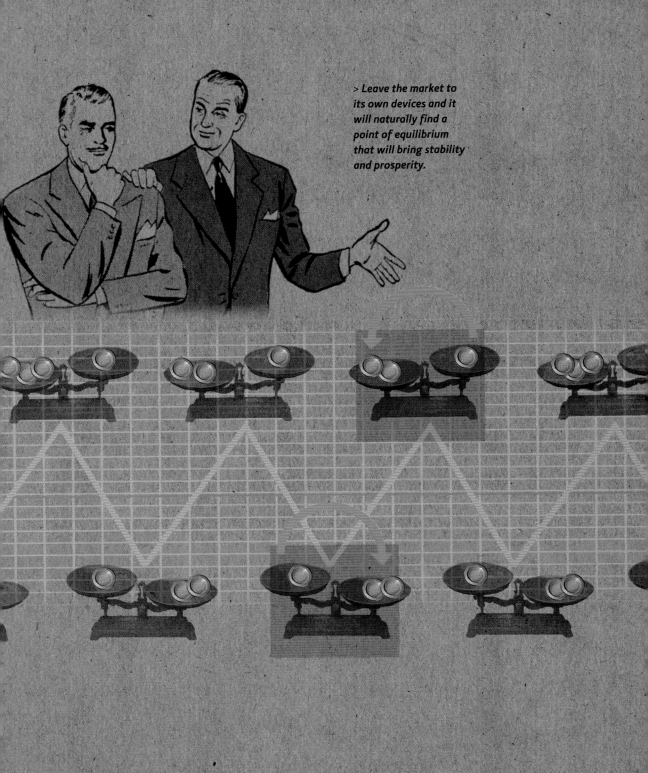

> Leave the market to its own devices and it will naturally find a point of equilibrium that will bring stability and prosperity.

MARXISM

the 30-second theory

Writing in the shadow of the nineteenth-century Industrial Revolution, Marx sought to unravel modern industrial capitalism. He argued that every commodity – an item produced for sale – has both a use value and an exchange value. For example, a chair has both a use (it provides a comfortable place to read this book) and an exchange – or monetary – value (it cost more than you had hoped from the furniture shop). Marx used this insight to argue that labour, too, is a commodity and is integral to the growth of capitalism. The labourer's use value is the ability to produce commodities, and in return the labourer is provided with a fair exchange value, or wage, which meets his basic costs of living. Yet when the labourer's use value is combined with the machines owned by the employer, the commodities produced are worth more than the labourer's exchange value; in this way a surplus is generated, which the employer takes as profit – this, Marx argued, is 'exploitation'. Such profit then provides the means by which capitalism can grow and expand, powered by the continual expansion of exploitation. Marx claimed that such an expansion also produced the antagonisms within such a system that would eventually lead the workers to seize control of the means of production – the machines and the factories – and establish a socialist economy.

3-SECOND CRASH
Capitalism requires profit and profit requires exploitation. But can exploitation produce socialism?

3-MINUTE BOOM
The fall of the Berlin Wall in 1989 and the collapse of the Soviet Union are seen by many to have wholly discredited Marxism. Yet how can Marxism make a positive contribution to our understanding of the modern capitalist economy? If we look beyond the legacy of dictatorship offered by the Soviet years, Marx's critique of capitalism can provide one starting point for understanding the inequities that still persist.

RELATED THEORIES
See also
MARKET SOCIALISM
page 30
CENTRAL PLANNING
page 34

3-SECOND BIOGRAPHIES
KARL MARX
1818–1883
FRIEDRICH ENGELS
1820–1895
ERNEST MANDEL
1923–1995
ANTONIO GRAMSCI
1891–1937

30-SECOND TEXT
Adam Fishwick

'In one word, for exploitation, veiled by religious and political illusions, [capitalism] has substituted naked, shameless, direct, brutal exploitation.'
KARL MARX

> *Marxism concludes that the inequalities brought about by capitalism will eventually lead to the workers seizing control in order to establish a socialist economy.*

KEYNESIAN ECONOMICS (POSITIVE)

the 30-second theory

Economic growth is not a steady process. The long-term trend has been upward, at least in developed economies, but in the short term economic growth is punctuated by what economists call the business cycle. There are booms of economic activity when growth accelerates and employment is high; but there are also downturns, when economies contract, jobs become scarce and unemployment rises. But what determines the extent of these swings? Classical economics affirmed that prices – including wages – respond quickly to changes in supply and demand, and that markets would, therefore, adjust rapidly to shocks. In classical theory, therefore, the business cycle shouldn't result in mass involuntary unemployment. But John Maynard Keynes, looking back on the Great Depression, argued against this. He said that aggregate demand – the total effective demand in an economy – was a key driver of the business cycle. During a downturn, aggregate demand tended to drop, which made the cycle worse, leading to prolonged periods of unnecessary unemployment. This idea then led Keynes and his followers to conclude that by manipulating aggregate demand, governments might be able to influence the business cycle, smoothing it out and reducing the volatility of capitalist development.

3-SECOND CRASH
Business cycles are driven by how much people are prepared to spend. When demand falls, recessions follow.

3-MINUTE BOOM
This demand-side perspective focuses on an important aspect of the way economies work. But that can't be the end of the story. Aggregate demand isn't the only thing that determines the way the economy functions; in the long run, for example, investment and innovation are key. And once you've suggested that governments might be able to manipulate aggregate demand as a way to manage the economy, the theory doesn't specify how – via monetary policy or fiscal? Nor does it mean that they have the means to do that sufficiently well.

RELATED THEORIES
See also
MONETARISM
page 48
SUPPLY-SIDE ECONOMICS
page 128
KEYNESIAN ECONOMICS (NORMATIVE)
page 46

3-SECOND BIOGRAPHIES
JOHN MAYNARD KEYNES
1883–1946
JOHN HICKS
1904–1989

30-SECOND TEXT
Christakis Georgiou

'The outstanding faults of the economic society in which we live are its failure to provide for full employment and its arbitrary and inequitable distribution of wealth and incomes.'
JOHN MAYNARD KEYNES

> *An economy in general may be growing, but there'll be intermittent financial storms – government intervention can help weather these.*

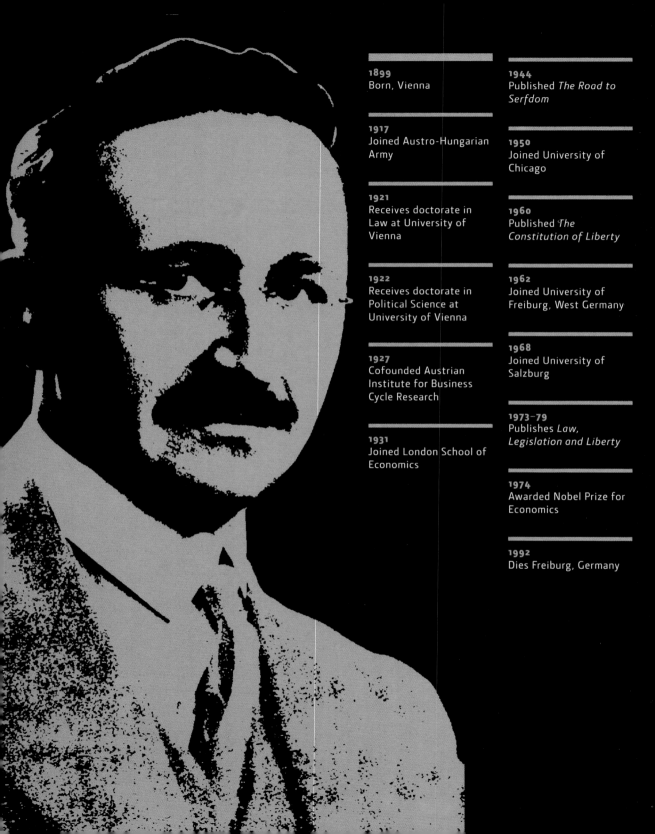

1899
Born, Vienna

1917
Joined Austro-Hungarian Army

1921
Receives doctorate in Law at University of Vienna

1922
Receives doctorate in Political Science at University of Vienna

1927
Cofounded Austrian Institute for Business Cycle Research

1931
Joined London School of Economics

1944
Published *The Road to Serfdom*

1950
Joined University of Chicago

1960
Published *The Constitution of Liberty*

1962
Joined University of Freiburg, West Germany

1968
Joined University of Salzburg

1973–79
Publishes *Law, Legislation and Liberty*

1974
Awarded Nobel Prize for Economics

1992
Dies Freiburg, Germany

FRIEDRICH VON HAYEK

One of the defining moments

of Margaret Thatcher's rise to power took place in the summer of 1975, a few months after she had been elected leader of the Conservative Party. Invited to attend a lecture on the 'middle way' at the Conservative Research Department, she reached into her bag and slammed a book on the table, saying, 'This is what we believe in.' The book was *The Constitution of Liberty* by Friedrich von Hayek. Nine years later, having provided the inspiration for half a decade of Thatcherism, Hayek was awarded the Order of the Companions of Honour by Queen Elizabeth II. This was followed by the Presidential Medal of Freedom, one of the top civilian awards in the United States, awarded by George Bush Sr in 1991. It was an unexpected and belated triumph for the man whose ideas seemed to have been comprehensively refuted by John Maynard Keynes half a century before.

Hayek was born in Vienna, Austria, in 1899 to a prominent family of academics. His parents were both members of the Austrian nobility, and his second cousin was the philosopher Ludwig Wittgenstein. Hayek started his own career studying brain anatomy, along with classes in law, political science, philosophy, psychology, and economics. He cofounded the Austrian Institute for Business Cycle Research in the 1920s and was subsequently recruited to the London School of Economics. He would remain there for the next 18 years, becoming a British subject in 1938. The British were already under the spell of Keynesianism, however, and Hayek struggled to get his message across. His solution was to write *The Road to Serfdom*, in which he argued that government intervention leads to less freedom and advocated a more 'laissez-faire' approach to economics. The book achieved moderate success in Britain but was later published to greater acclaim in the United States, where he lived from 1950. He spent his latter years in Germany and Austria, and was still writing stinging critiques of socialism well into his late eighties.

NEOCLASSICAL SYNTHESIS

the 30-second theory

The experience of the Great

Depression of the 1930s and the impact of Keynes' work had a lasting influence on economic theory. As early as 1937, John Hicks, a Cambridge economist, tried to present a mathematical version of Keynes' arguments, which then became the basis of the so-called 'post-war synthesis' of Keynesianism and classical economics. An MIT professor and Nobelist, Paul Samuelson was the most prominent 'neo-Keynesian'. The gist of the synthesis was that, in the short term, markets could be imperfect and therefore did not always clear or adjust as predicted by the classical models. This was mainly due to the rigidity of wages and the distorting impact monopolies had on competition. The government could, therefore, intervene in order to fix these imperfections. For example, the government might boost its spending in times of weakness, moving the economy towards full employment. But once this was done, there was no reason to discard the key idea that markets clear and arrive at equilibrium. Or that in the long run it was the expansion of productive capacity that determined an economy's growth. If governments intervened correctly, then once any market imperfections were corrected, the invisible hand of the market would work its wonders once again.

RELATED THEORIES
See also
KEYNESIAN ECONOMICS
(POSITIVE)
page 16
CLASSICAL
page 12

3-SECOND BIOGRAPHIES
JOHN HICKS
1904–1989

PAUL SAMUELSON
1915–

30-SECOND TEXT
Christakis Georgiou

3-SECOND CRASH
Keynes was right about the short term but the classicals were right about the long term. Government intervention should be limited to the short term.

3-MINUTE BOOM
Most of Keynes' students at Cambridge University, objected to the 'post-war synthesis'. They said that it restored the main idea that Keynes had tried to refute – that markets are self-regulating. Because of this, the neo-Keynesians had adapted the pre-1930s idea that unemployment was due to high wages whereas Keynes had tried to show this idea was wrong because cutting wages had deepened the slump instead of solving the problem.

'Years ago, economists used to regard perfect competition as the ideal ... Today, we realize that all the world is an exception to perfect competition. Were we to chop off the head of everyone who is an imperfect competitor, there would be few heads left.'

PAUL SAMUELSON

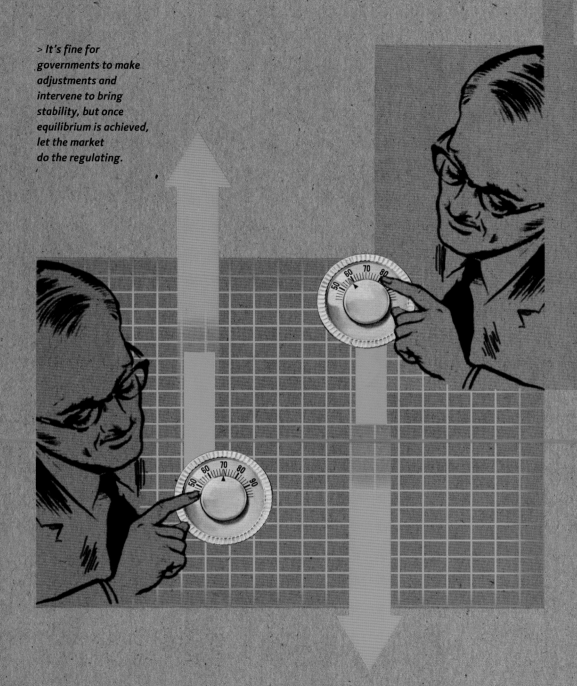

> It's fine for governments to make adjustments and intervene to bring stability, but once equilibrium is achieved, let the market do the regulating.

AUSTRIAN SCHOOL
the 30-second theory

Before the First World War,

Vienna was one of the most important places for economic theory. Some of the most important marginalists, such as Carl Menger and Eugen von Böhm-Bawerk, taught at the University of Vienna. But the most famous 'Austrians' are Ludwig von Mises and Friedrich von Hayek. Between the First and Second World Wars, and after the Second World War, they argued that socialism either ruled out rational calculation altogether (Mises) or that it could only be an inferior system to capitalism because it was far less efficient (Hayek). Their argument was that only individuals have the ability to determine their own costs and benefits, because these are entirely subjective. This means that the most efficient way of organizing economic activity is to allow the market to spontaneously coordinate between the preferences of the myriad consumers in society. Prices then perform the most important role in an economy because they reflect all the disparate information in the economy. But this can only be achieved by a laissez-faire approach. In socialism, the state intervenes to set prices, but because it cannot possibly possess all the information regarding costs and preferences available in society, it will inevitably make a mess of the job.

RELATED THEORIES
See also
MARGINALISM
page 138

FREE MARKET CAPITALISM
page 28

MARKET SOCIALISM
page 30

3-SECOND BIOGRAPHIES
CARL MENGER
1840–1921

EUGEN VON BÖHM-BAWERK
1851–1914

LUDWIG VON MISES
1881–1973

FRIEDRICH VON HAYEK
1899–1992

30-SECOND TEXT
Christakis Georgiou

3-SECOND CRASH
Only individuals know how they value things and only the market can coordinate efficiently everyone's preferences. No government can know better than the market.

3-MINUTE BOOM
The ideas of the 'Austrians' remained in the margin of economics until the early 1980s, when they found an echo in some of the policies of Ronald Reagan and Margaret Thatcher. The 'Austrians' are the strongest opponents of government intervention and are considered the fathers of right-wing libertarianism. But their insistence on the superiority of absolute laissez-faire seems far-fetched. It seems too much to argue that a society will only function properly if no collective decisions are taken.

'The economic problem of society ... to put it briefly, is a problem of the utilization of knowledge not given to anyone in its totality.'
FRIEDRICH VON HAYEK

> Only a free market is able to effectively coordinate all the information and attitudes each individual has in regard to value – in this way market prices are reached.

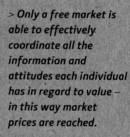

ECONOMIC SYSTEMS

ECONOMIC SYSTEMS
GLOSSARY

capitalism An economic system whereby the means of production (factories, machinery and so on) and distribution are owned primarily by private individuals or corporations. The prices of labour and goods are determined on the free market, and not by central government. Profits are claimed by individual company owners or, in the case of corporations, distributed to shareholders.

deregulation The process of removing government controls from the market and increasing free trade, the idea being that the less intervention from government, the more dynamic and competitive the market. Typical government controls include a minimum wage, tariffs on imports, and currency controls.

globalization The process through which restrictions to international trade are removed and companies trade freely across national boundaries. The process is usually accompanied by increased outsourcing, whereby individual stages of production are allocated to companies in different countries, according to price, resulting in a massive increase in transportation.

hyperinflation Literally, what it sounds like: very high inflation! Most economists describe an increase in prices of 50 per cent per month as hyperinflation, although the term is often used to describe much lower rates. The classic example is Germany in the 1920s, when inflation reached 322 per cent and prices quadrupled every month.

International Monetary Fund (IMF)
The IMF was created in 1944 as part of the Bretton Woods negotiations. Its main purpose is to help countries stabilize their balance of payments (that is import/export balance) by giving loans to those in deficit. In return, however, it imposes stringent conditions – often referred to as the Washington Consensus – designed to liberalize markets and reduce government intervention. Based in Washington, D.C., it currently boasts 186 members.

kleptocracy A government in which corruption is endemic; taxes and other government funds are used for the personal profit of officials, at the expense of the wider populace. The most famous case is the Philippines' government under Marcos, when the country's treasury was used virtually as a personal bank account.

neoliberalism A strand of economic thinking based on neoclassical theories, first expounded by David Ricardo and developed by Milton Friedman et al. The principal policies are a reduction of state intervention in favour of private initiatives, governed by an open and free market. More specifically, neoliberals believe in privatizing government assets, reducing government spending, reducing tax, and removing barriers to trade (such as licensing, tariffs, quotas, and so on).

protectionism The practice of protecting the domestic market against foreign competition by imposing quotas and tariffs on incoming goods. This is usually done to ensure a positive balance of payments, where imports of foreign goods threaten to outweigh exports of locally-produced goods. It may also be done to protect a nascent industry, such as car manufacturing in Japan in the 1930s and 1940s.

socialism An economic system whereby the means of production and distribution are owned by the workers or by the state. Prices of goods and wages are determined by central government instead of being determined by the market (although some forms of socialism do incorporate the market mechanism). The whole economy is rationally planned, rather than being determined by the random outcome of private initiatives.

World Bank Like the IMF (above), the World Bank was created during the Bretton Woods Conference to assist the post-war economic recovery. Unlike the IMF, however, it grants loans for specific development projects. Increasingly, the Bank has focused on reducing poverty in the developing world, although its policies are often blamed for forcing debtor nations to adopt liberal policies that leave them open to exploitation by multinational corporations.

FREE MARKET CAPITALISM

the 30-second theory

3-SECOND CRASH
Free markets and private ownership will result in maximum prosperity and freedom for all.

3-MINUTE BOOM
Free market capitalism assumes that if we allow private individuals to act with limited regulation, maximum prosperity will spread to all. Yet Marx argues that such a system results in the exploitation of the mass of the population to the benefit of a narrow few. With inequality and poverty rife within and across countries throughout the world, is it the case that markets are not simply 'free enough', or was Marx right?

Milton Friedman famously argued that for capitalism to flourish the state must remove itself from all economic activity except for 'the military, the courts and some of the major highways'. This free market capitalism is based upon the central premise that private individuals rather than state regulators make the best economic decisions. For example, the business owner will make investments carefully in order to best satisfy his customers. An individual worker, meanwhile, will choose among jobs based on the hours, the pay and the skills he or she may develop. All economic actors seek their most beneficial opportunities, and, in doing so, help move the economy towards maximum prosperity. The role of the state in the economy is thus reduced to that of the 'night watchman', playing a very minor role in facilitating this activity – protecting private property rights, maintaining law and order, and defending the system from external aggression. As a corollary, free trade is promoted for the international economy to ensure maximum prosperity across the globe. Allowing private individuals to freely trade across borders without state restrictions enables each nation to make best use of its comparative advantage, whether it's growing coffee beans or making computers.

RELATED THEORIES
See also
CLASSICAL
page 12
MONETARISM
page 48
COMPARATIVE ADVANTAGE
page 88

3-SECOND BIOGRAPHIES
ADAM SMITH
1723–1790

MILTON FRIEDMAN
1912–2006

30-SECOND TEXT
Adam Fishwick

'It is necessary in the first instance that the parties in the market should be free to sell and buy at any price at which they can find a partner to the transaction, and that anybody should be free to produce, sell, and buy anything that may be produced or sold at all.'
FRIEDRICH VON HAYEK

> Free market capitalists argue that it's individuals and not the state who are best equipped to make economic decisions – companies should be free to trade any commodity without restrictions.

MARKET SOCIALISM

the 30-second theory

RELATED THEORY
See also
FREE MARKET CAPITALISM
page 28

3-SECOND BIOGRAPHIES
ENRICO BARONE
1859–1924

OSKAR R. LANGE
1904–1965

30-SECOND TEXT
Christakis Georgiou

3-SECOND CRASH
The state owns the means of production and sets prices but firms are run by their own managers. It's the best of both worlds.

3-MINUTE BOOM
The theory sounds great. What could be better than combining the rationality of the market with 'collective' ownership of the means of production? But then how is this system different from straightforward free market capitalism? If firms compete against each other on the marketplace and investment decisions are left to them, does it make a difference whether formally they belong to the state or not? They are still driven by profit making.

Can you combine the market and state ownership of the means of production? Some economists stand by a tradition that considers you can, and that this provides the best of both worlds. In the traditional and theoretical model, developed by the Italian economist Enrico Barone and further explored by the Polish economist Oskar R. Lange, the state owns the means of production and a central authority determines prices by trial and error. If there's a surplus, it lowers prices; if there's a shortage, it raises them. What's more, most firms have a considerable amount of freedom on how they will be run and the role of central planning is very weak – but the state, however, still makes the important infrastructural investment decisions. This way, both the principle of state ownership of the means of production and the efficiency of the market mechanism coexist. This model has never been applied as such, although some Soviet-style economies, including the USSR under Mikhail Gorbachev, attempted in the 1970s and 1980s to adopt its main idea, by limiting central planning and allowing individual state-owned firms managerial autonomy. Today, China – since the late 1970s under Teng Hsiao-p'ing – Vietnam, and Laos are the economies that come closest to market socialism, although they have a significant private sector and no price-setting authority.

'Planning and market forces are not the essential difference between socialism and capitalism. A planned economy is not the definition of socialism, because there is planning under capitalism; the market economy happens under socialism, too. Planning and market forces are both ways of controlling economic activity.'
TENG HSIAO-P'ING

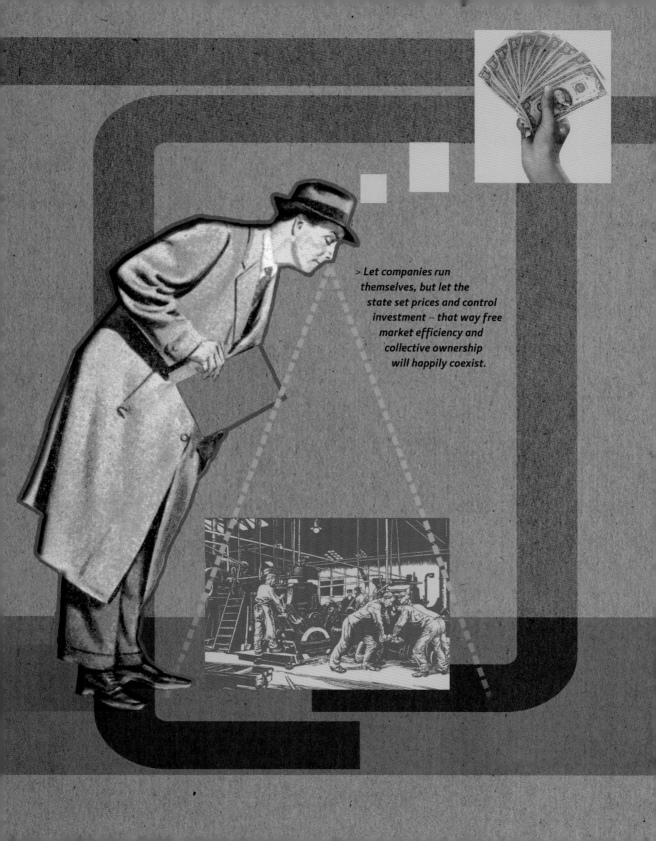

> Let companies run themselves, but let the state set prices and control investment – that way free market efficiency and collective ownership will happily coexist.

1912
Born, Brooklyn, New York

1933
MA, University of
Chicago

1937
Joins National Bureau of
Economic Research

1946
Professor in Economic
Theory at University of
Chicago

1963
Publishes *A Monetary
History of the United
States, 1867–1960*

1976
Awarded Nobel Prize in
Economics

1982
Publishes *Capitalism and
Freedom*

1988
Awarded Presidential
Medal of Freedom by
Ronald Reagan

2006
Dies, San Francisco

MILTON FRIEDMAN

So who is the most influential economist of the second half of the twentieth century? According to *The Economist* magazine, that honour goes to Milton Friedman. Certainly his staunch defence of the free market did have a major influence on the economic and social life of the modern world. His theories of government deregulation provided the intellectual basis for the governments of Ronald Reagan, Margaret Thatcher, and, perhaps less gloriously, August Pinochet in Chile. Indeed, it could be argued that his theories provided the intellectual underpinnings of the entire neoliberal project, including the so-called 'Washington Consensus', with all its global repercussions. Friedman was so committed to deregulation that he advocated the legalization of marijuana and prostitution. He believed that doctors' licenses encouraged a monopoly of the profession and discouraged competition. He was a fervent opponent of the draft – which he said ran against the principles of individual freedom – and believed so strongly in the voucher system of education that he set up his own institute to promote the concept. He also opposed the welfare system and advocated a 'negative income tax' (in the form of tax credits) to replace it. Whatever else he might be accused of, Friedman was consistent in his beliefs.

Born in New York in 1912 to recently emigrated Jewish parents, Friedman was initially a supporter of Keynesian economics. He would later reverse that theory with the publication in 1963 of *A Monetary History of the United States, 1867–1960*, which argued that monetary policy was the most important factor in achieving economic stability. From 1946, Friedman taught at the University of Chicago, where he formed the influential Chicago School of Economics, which, for the next 30 years, produced a steady stream of Nobel Prize winners. He advised Ronald Reagan during his successful 1980 presidential campaign, before going on to serve on the Economic Policy Advisory Board. He and his wife Rose became household names when their ten-part TV series *Free to Choose* was broadcast on US television in 1980.

CENTRAL PLANNING

the 30-second theory

3-SECOND CRASH
The state controls all the machines and factories and makes all investment decisions. There is no role for market forces here.

3-MINUTE BOOM
It is very widely held that the command economies of the Eastern bloc and China were the socialism Marx had talked about. But when you look at Marx's version of socialism, this proves to be wrong. For Marx, socialism meant that workers controlled the means of production themselves, not the state, and accordingly decided among themselves what to produce and how to distribute it. In this one respect, socialism would view capitalism and command economies as similar.

The Cold War is now history.

But as long as it existed, it was the most important reference in debates among economists or political scientists. On the one hand there existed 'capitalism' and on the other, 'communism'. In communist countries, production and distribution were dominated by the state, which owned and controlled machines, factories and shops. A central government body would meet every few years – usually five – and come up with a plan of what to produce, how, when, and for what purpose. It then distributed the tasks to factory managers and set them targets. Because production was planned in this system by a central authority and then orders were handed out, it became known as central planning. This system was supposed to be socialist because the economy was planned and a free market or private enterprise didn't exist. Proponents favoured this approach because command economies were regarded as more efficient in terms of 'catching up' with the West. Wholly planned economies along these lines existed in most Eastern bloc countries and in China until the 1970s. After which a wave of liberalization either transformed these command economies to 'market socialism' (as in China for example) or ended up destroying 'communism' altogether (as in Eastern Europe and Russia).

RELATED THEORIES
See also
FREE MARKET CAPITALISM
page 28
MARKET SOCIALISM
page 30

3-SECOND BIOGRAPHIES
JOSEPH STALIN
1878–1953

MAO TSE-TUNG
1893–1976

30-SECOND TEXT
Christakis Georgiou

'We are fifty or a hundred years behind the advanced countries. We must make good this distance in ten years. Either we do it, or they will crush us.'
JOSEPH STALIN

> Decisions about what to produce and how to produce it are made centrally – there's no room for a free market here.

MERCANTILISM
the 30-second theory

3-SECOND CRASH
Keep the foreigners out and your money in and make sure you always sell abroad more than you buy – it's nationalism for the economy.

3-MINUTE BOOM
To proponents of free trade, mercantilism just doesn't add up. The strongest opponents of mercantilism have been classical and Austrian school economists. They accused mercantilists of not understanding the benefits of free trade and the impossibility for a country to always sell abroad more than it buys. The Austrian economists accused it of being an imperialist doctrine, the aim of which was to build strong state power. But today, neomercantilists are generally the ones who criticize rich and powerful countries rather than the other way around.

To get a national economy to develop quickly and to catch up with more advanced nations, you need the government to intervene heavily in the economy to protect local industry and firms by protectionist measures, such as tariffs and subsidies. You also need to limit as much as possible the import of goods and services and the export of capital; in other words, you need to sell foreigners more things than they sell you and you must keep and invest your money in your own country. Mercantilism was the most popular economic doctrine between the sixteenth and eighteenth centuries. Its most prominent exponent at the time was the French statesman Jean-Baptiste Colbert. The system went on to inform nineteenth-century American and German economic policy, while also playing a role in the development of Japan and other East Asian nations such as Taiwan, South Korea, Singapore, Hong Kong, and especially China during the late twentieth century. In today's world, mercantilism mostly goes by the name of economic nationalism or as the theory of export-oriented growth. Many critical economists, such as Ha-Joon Chang, use mercantilism to criticize globalization. He argues that globalization and the free market have 'kicked away the ladder' of state intervention and protectionism that rich countries once used to develop strong economies from beneath the feet of today's poor and developing countries.

RELATED THEORY
See also
CLASSICAL
page 12

3-SECOND BIOGRAPHY
JEAN-BAPTISTE COLBERT
1619–1683

30-SECOND TEXT
Christakis Georgiou

'Almost all of today's rich countries used tariff protection and subsidies to develop their industries. Interestingly, Britain and the USA, the two countries that are supposed to have reached the summit of the world economy through their free-market, free-trade policy, are actually the ones that had most aggressively used protection and subsidies.'

HA-JOON CHANG

> Export more than
you import – with the
help of government
subsidies and tariffs –
and invest at home and
your national economy
will quickly prosper.

SHOCK THERAPY

the 30-second theory

When a country is in economic crisis, some believe the best way to fix it is all at once – a method called 'shock therapy'. For a government-controlled economy that's suffering from chronic food shortages or hyperinflation, for example, the solution is radical change. Get government out, and fast, even if it hurts in the short term. If countries liberalize – that is, they drop price and currency controls, take away state subsidies, open borders to free trade, find new revenue sources to close budget gaps, and privatize government-owned businesses – markets can work properly, goods appear in the shops, and inflation slows or reverses. As Jeffrey Sachs, a key architect of shock therapy, says, you can't cross a chasm in two jumps. Germany used shock therapy between 1947 and 1948, when government suddenly dropped price controls and subsidies. Goods reappeared, poverty receded, and Germany quickly became a developed market economy. The term was coined, however, when it saved Bolivia's economy in 1985. It also worked in Poland, whose economy has largely caught up with western Europe's since shock therapy was used in 1990. However, it doesn't always work: in post-Soviet Russia, privatization led to massive corruption when people grabbed for lucrative gas and oil ownership.

RELATED THEORIES
See also
CLASSICAL
page 12
FREE MARKET CAPITALISM
page 28
CENTRAL PLANNING
page 34
THE WASHINGTON CONSENSUS
page 40

3-SECOND BIOGRAPHIES
JEFFREY SACHS
1954–

GONZALO SÁNCHEZ DE LOZADA
1930–

LESZEK BALCEROWICZ
1947–

30-SECOND TEXT
Katie Huston

3-SECOND CRASH
The best way to fix a broken economy is in one fell swoop.

3-MINUTE BOOM
Is it really best – or even possible – to change an economy from government-run to market-oriented overnight? Critics say change should be more gradual, and point to China's success as an example. Others argue that even if it worked in Bolivia and Poland, it might not work elsewhere. To liberalize, a country needs a restructured economy and a framework of law and regulation that doesn't spring up overnight. When that framework is missing, as in post-Soviet Russia, reform may lead to kleptocracy rather than a functioning market economy.

'Inflation is like a tiger and you have only one shot; if you don't get it with that one shot, it'll get you.'
GONZALO SÁNCHEZ DE LOZADA

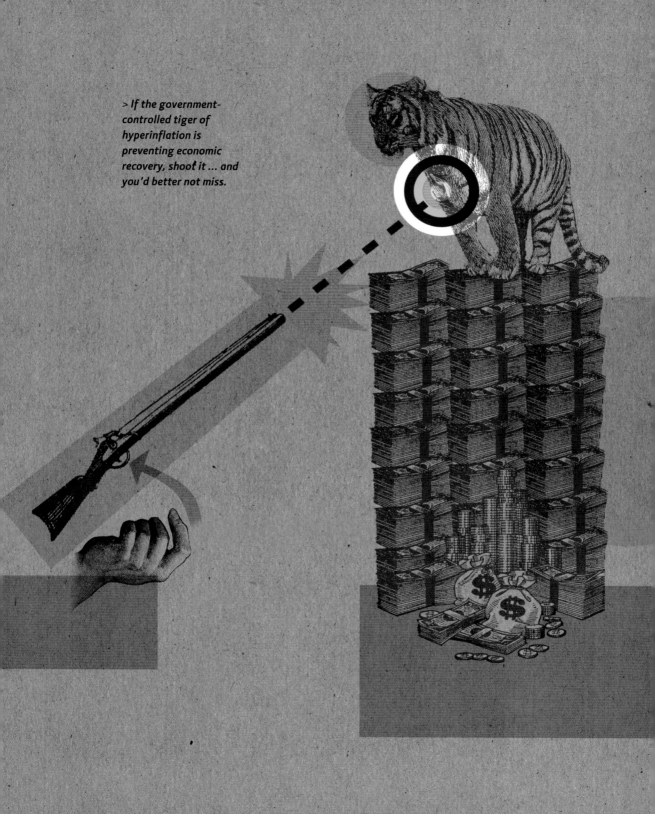

> If the government-controlled tiger of hyperinflation is preventing economic recovery, shoot it ... and you'd better not miss.

THE WASHINGTON CONSENSUS

the 30-second theory

Stabilize, privatize, liberalize,
globalize – and balance your budget. It's the wise thing to do, or so claims the Washington Consensus. The term was coined by economist John Williamson in 1989 to describe a set of policy recommendations for developing countries. According to the big boys in Washington – the World Bank, the International Monetary Fund, and the US Treasury – the key to development was deregulation and fiscal discipline. Stabilize: keep inflation down, reduce trade deficits, and keep the money supply in check. Privatize: turn public goods, such as water, over to private companies to improve efficiency. Liberalize: open your borders to free trade and attract foreign direct investment. Deregulate: don't limit competition or try to keep players out of the market. And stick to fiscal discipline: don't let government spend more than it brings in. These policies were designed with Latin America in mind, but soon they were applied in other regions. Poor states that took IMF loans were forced to satisfy conditions, known as structural adjustment policies: stabilize, privatize and so on. These programs have come under heavy fire as a 'one-size-fits-all' remedy for countries that are anything but the same, an adjustment program that does more harm than good – and a program the rich countries fail to follow

RELATED THEORY
see also
COMPARATIVE ADVANTAGE
page 88

3-SECOND BIOGRAPHIES
JOHN WILLIAMSON
1937–
MILTON FRIEDMAN
1912–2006

30-SECOND TEXT
Katie Huston

3-SECOND CRASH
Keep your controls open and your government small and business will grow and grow and grow.

3-MINUTE BOOM
The phrase 'Washington Consensus' is often used interchangeably with 'neoliberalism' – and blamed for everything that's gone wrong in the developing world. But Williamson argues that they're not the same. The Washington Consensus may be a damaged brand name, he says, but in some cases its ideas worked – for example, when Argentina privatized the water supply, infant mortality in the poorest areas decreased by 24 per cent.

'For the most part [the basic ideas] are motherhood and apple pie, which is why they commanded a consensus.'
JOHN WILLIAMSON

> *Reduce regulation from government and give free enterprise the power to prosper for the benefit of all.*

ECONOMIC CYCLES

aggregate demand The total demand for goods and services within an economy at a certain time. This can be influenced by government either through monetary policy (that is, controlling the amount of money in the economy through interest rates and other means) and/or fiscal policy (that is, increasing/decreasing the amount of government expenditure).

balance of payments The difference between the total spent on goods and services imported from overseas and the amount earned from goods and services sold overseas. Countries often aim to export more than they import, to give them a balance of payments surplus. Since the early 1980s, however, the United States has run a balance of payments deficit of up to 6 per cent of gross domestic product (GDP) without grinding to a halt.

credit crunch A restriction on the availability of credit, or loans. This is often the result of a loss of confidence in a sector of the finance market, leading investors to withdraw their funds to invest in a safer option.

expansionary policies If an economy is in recession, a government may adopt expansionary policies to attempt to reinvigorate it. These can include monetary policies, such as reducing interest rates and buying bonds to increase the amount of money in the system. They can also include fiscal policies, such as investing heavily in public services, building projects, or cutting taxes.

inflation The increase in the price of goods and services over a given period of time, usually measured using the Consumer Price Index. A small amount of inflation is generally regarded as acceptable because it helps to smooth relative price adjustments in the economy. Very high inflation, however, leads to instability in the financial markets and worker unrest as the real value of wages drops.

money supply This refers to the total amount of money in circulation within an economy at a given point in time. This can be controlled by central government partly by raising or lowering interest rates – high interest rates usually means less money in the system; low interest rates means more – but also through other policies, such as the purchase of long-term bonds, to inject a quantity of cash (known as 'quantitative easing').

'Ponzi' borrower A person who takes out a loan to buy an asset and is dependent on the appreciation (increase in value) of that asset to pay off the interest and original sum of the loan. The term was invented by Hyman Minsky and contrasts with other types of borrowers who repay debts using moneys earned from investments. The Ponzi type of borrower was quite common right before the 2007 subprime crisis, as the spiralling price of property lulled buyers into thinking they could pay off their debts using the equity in their houses.

private sector That part of the economy owned and run by individuals and corporations mostly (but not always) for profit.

public sector That part of the economy owned and run by the state. Typically, this will include provision of social security, education, defence, public transport, and certain utilities. These may or may not be run for profit.

stagflation Literally, a combination of stagnation and inflation. Until the 1970s, most economists believed it was impossible to have both at the same time, and much of Keynesian theory was based on this assumption. The advent of stagflation in the 1970s meant that governments could no longer spend their way out of recession without risking unacceptably high inflation. As a result, Keynesian policies were marginalized for the next three decades.

supply-siders Those who believe that economic prosperity is dependent on creating the best conditions possible for the suppliers of products and services (that is the employers). Thus, regulation should be kept to a minimum and corporate taxes should be as low as possible. Demand-siders believe that empowering workers and encouraging them to consume more creates demand for products, which in turn stimulates industry and creates employment. Thus, governments should invest in educating and creating opportunities for workers and ensuring they get a fair deal from employers through employment legislation.

KEYNESIAN ECONOMICS (NORMATIVE)

the 30-second theory

3-SECOND CRASH
The government should spend and cut taxes to soften economic downturns.

3-MINUTE BOOM
Keynesianism seemed to be the cure to capitalism's problems. For 30 years, growth rates were high and most people had a job – in the West at least. But in the 1970s there was stagflation and government spending couldn't make things better. The monetarists attacked Keynesians, suggesting that governments had overexpanded the money supply, so creating inflation. Supply-siders pointed out that expanding the supply-side would both increase production and bring inflation down.

John Maynard Keynes diagnosed the Great Depression as a failure of aggregate demand: people didn't want to spend, and so the world economy spiralled downwards. His prescription? The government should boost aggregate demand. In particular, it should boost its own spending to fill the gap in aggregate demand from the private sector. By spending on new projects, making transfers to people in need or cutting taxes, the government could boost demand. Firms would then employ more workers to produce more. Those workers would spend their earnings, and you would have a virtuous cycle of growth that would get the economy out of the recession and reduce unemployment. Keynesianism became the most popular economic doctrine of the 'golden age' of capitalism (1945–1973). The key idea was that governments have to intervene in the economy to ensure full employment; if the rate of unemployment was left to the free market, it would naturally run much higher. Government intervention took the form of public spending, tax cuts for workers, and transfer payments.

RELATED THEORIES
See also
CLASSICAL
page 12
AUSTRIAN SCHOOL
page 22
MONETARISM
page 48
SUPPLY-SIDE ECONOMICS
page 128
KEYNESIAN ECONOMICS (POSITIVE)
page 16

3-SECOND BIOGRAPHIES
JOHN MAYNARD KEYNES
1883–1946
JOHN KENNETH GALBRAITH
1908–2006

30-SECOND TEXT
Christakis Georgiou

'The government should pay people to dig holes in the ground and then fill them up.'
JOHN MAYNARD KEYNES

> *If governments introduce money into the economy, it will stimulate production, and so lead to full employment.*

MONETARISM

the 30-second theory

As its name suggests, monetarism is primarily concerned with monetary policy. Its role in controlling the supply of money into the economy is claimed to be the single most important factor influencing short- and long-term economic changes. In the short term, individual decisions regarding consumption and investment are affected by changes in the money supply. Increases in the money supply will encourage spending and thus boost economic activity, while decreases will reduce it. Such a statement may appear as common sense – control over how much money is in the economy will surely influence economic behaviour. Effective monetary policy, however, stabilizes prices without affecting individual output and consumption in the long term. Unstable price growth will only result in market distortions, sacrificing low inflation and steady growth for short-lived gains in output and consumption. High inflation should be addressed by reducing the supply of money into the economy, with the long-term benefits of stability outweighing any short-term costs. Yet excessive restrictions upon the supply of money should be avoided, with Milton Friedman and Anna Schwartz famously blaming such a situation for the Great Depression in 1929. Ultimately, a controlled and constant increase of the money supply will keep inflation low while expanding economic activity and employment.

3-SECOND CRASH
Control your money and the rest will follow!

3-MINUTE BOOM
The application of monetarist policy is often associated with a significant reduction in the money supply as a means to reduce growing inflation rates. The argument is that in the long term, stability and growth will result, as happened after the United States' successful battle against inflation in the early 1980s. Yet one corollary of this is a short-term increase in unemployment. Do such immediate social consequences outweigh the assumed benefits of such monetary policy?

RELATED THEORIES
See also
NEOCLASSICAL SYNTHESIS
page 20
FREE MARKET CAPITALISM
page 28
SHOCK THERAPY
page 38
THE WASHINGTON CONSENSUS
page 40

3-SECOND BIOGRAPHIES
MILTON FRIEDMAN
1912–2006

KARL BRUNNER
1916–1989

ANNA SCHWARTZ
1915–

30-SECOND TEXT
Adam Fishwick

'Inflation is always and everywhere a monetary phenomenon.'
MILTON FRIEDMAN

> Controlling the supply of money has a direct affect on the economy. Increase the supply to encourage growth, reduce it to control inflation.

1883
Born, Cambridge, UK

1904
BA in Mathematics,
King's College,
Cambridge

1908
Professor of Economics,
University of Cambridge

1915
Joins British Treasury

1919
Publishes *The Economic
Consequences of the
Peace*

1920
Professor of Economics,
University of Cambridge

1925
Marries Lydia Lopokova

1930
Publishes *A Treatise on
Money*

1933
Publishes *The Means to
Prosperity*

1936
Publishes *The General
Theory of Employment,
Interest and Money*

1942
Receives peerage from
King George VI

1944
Leads British delegation
at Bretton Woods

1946
Dies, East Sussex, UK

JOHN MAYNARD KEYNES

Few economists achieve such success that their name is given to an entire branch of the subject – Adam Smith didn't achieve that, nor did Alfred Marshall, and nor did Milton Friedman. Yet, even now, 60 years after its creator's death, the principles of Keynesianism are once again discussed almost daily on our television screens. So who was John Maynard Keynes, and why is he once again so influential?

Keynes came to public prominence during the Treaty of Versailles in 1919 when he spoke out against the punitive reparation payments being imposed by France and the United States, arguing that they would make it impossible for the German economy to recover. His predictions were proven correct, as the collapse of the Weimar Republic swept Hitler's National Socialist Party to power and, ultimately, led to the Second World War. But it was during the Great Depression that Keynes began to develop his most important ideas. Chief among these was the theory of countercyclical government spending – in other words, when the economy is in recession the government should spend to stimulate economic growth, and when the economy is doing well, government should spend less and save for the bad times. *The General Theory of Employment, Interest and Money* was published in 1936 and became an instant bestseller. His ideas prevailed after World War II, when Keynesian policies were adopted by governments around the world, leading to what is known the 'golden age' of economics. Despite falling out of favour in the 1970s and 1980s, his ideas have resurfaced recently in the 'stimulus packages' implemented by Barack Obama, Gordon Brown, and others.

Keynes, meanwhile, enjoyed a rich and varied life outside work. A member of the Bloomsbury Group, he had mainly homosexual relationships before marrying the Russian ballerina Lydia Lopokova in 1927. He was an enthusiastic art collector, accruing paintings by Cézanne, Degas, Modigliani, and Picasso. He was also a shrewd investor and, despite not foreseeing the stock market crash of 1929, had accumulated a small fortune by the time he died in April 1946.

THE PHILLIPS CURVE

the 30-second theory

3-SECOND CRASH
A government has to choose – low inflation or full employment, it can't have both. The Phillips curve shows the trade-off between the two.

3-MINUTE BOOM
The problem with this theory is that it can't explain what happened in the 1970s in most of the Western world. Wages and prices were rising very fast – there was high inflation – but unemployment was also rising and output was not growing very fast. The trade-off between inflation and unemployment was lost. Economists don't agree on why this happened. Almost all economists now believe that there is no Phillips curve in the long term, but that it does exist (with some modifications) over the short term.

New Zealand-born economist, Bill Phillips, wrote an article in 1958 comparing wage inflation (increases in nominal wages) and unemployment in the United Kingdom from 1861 to 1957. He observed that when wages rose quickly unemployment fell, and when unemployment rose, wage increases slowed down or even became negative (that is, wages dropped). Because price increases were approximately 2 per cent below wage increases in the same period, Phillips argued that there was a relationship between inflation and unemployment – if you have high inflation then you have low unemployment and vice versa. How is this important? It means that if a government accepts the Phillips curve, then it has a choice. If you want price stability, then make more people unemployed. If you want everyone to have a job, then you have to put up with prices increasing all the time. Governments can try and put into practice these choices by manipulating interest rates. If they raise them, then more people go on unemployment; if they keep them low, there is more investment and more people can be offered a job.

RELATED THEORIES
See also
MONETARISM
page 48
RATIONAL EXPECTATIONS
page 56
KEYNESIAN ECONOMICS
(NORMATIVE)
page 46
NEOCLASSICAL GROWTH
page 70

3-SECOND BIOGRAPHY
A. W. 'BILL' PHILLIPS
1914–1975

30-SECOND TEXT
Christakis Georgiou

'Inflation is like sin; every government denounces it and every government practices it.'
FREDERICK LEITH-ROSS

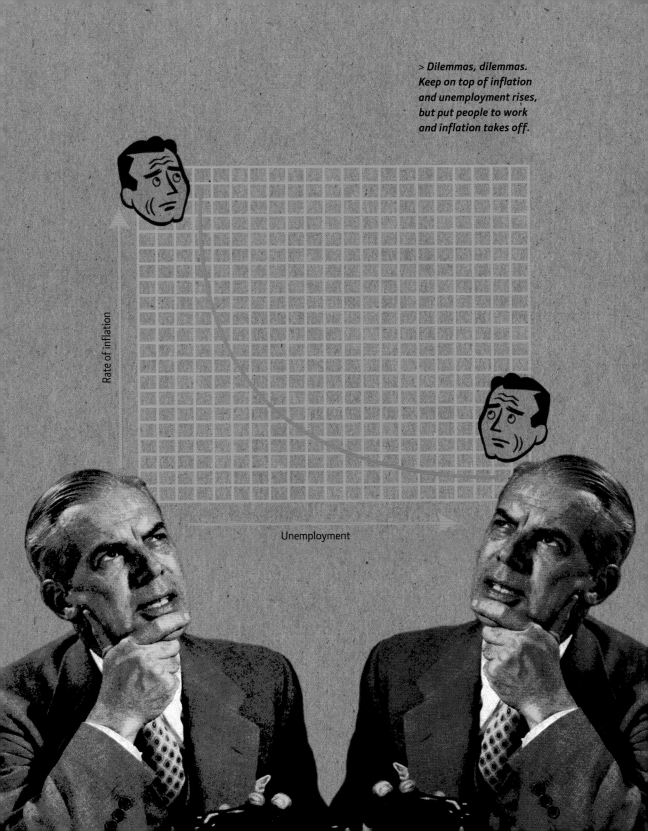

> Dilemmas, dilemmas. Keep on top of inflation and unemployment rises, but put people to work and inflation takes off.

Rate of inflation

Unemployment

PERMANENT INCOME HYPOTHESIS

the 30-second theory

In the late 1950s, Milton Friedman proposed that when considering what they can spend, most people assess what they are going to earn during their entire lifetime – their permanent income – as opposed to their economic circumstances at the time. How does this work? To estimate their permanent income, people look at their current income and envision how this is likely to evolve during their lifetime. On this basis, people take out loans that they repay over many years, put a part of their income on the side as savings, and spend the rest on day-to-day consumption. This implies that if, for some reason, people receive an unexpected rise in their temporary income, then they will save most of it rather than spend it right away, until it becomes clear whether this temporary increase will become a permanent one. The interesting aspect for government policy makers is that what applies to individuals invariably applies to the economy as a whole. Result? A temporary rise in national income will not sustainably boost demand. There's no point in governments using short-term, demand-boosting policies because they will not lift aggregate demand. People will just save the extra cash handed out by the government.

RELATED THEORIES
See also
RATIONAL EXPECTATIONS
page 56
KEYNESIAN ECONOMICS
(NORMATIVE)
page 46
SUPPLY-SIDE ECONOMICS
page 128

3-SECOND BIOGRAPHIES
MILTON FRIEDMAN
1912–2006

FRANCO MODIGLIANI
1918–2003

30-SECOND TEXT
Christakis Georgiou

'At the beginning of the cask and the end take thy fill but be saving in the middle; for at the bottom the savings comes too late.'
HESIOD

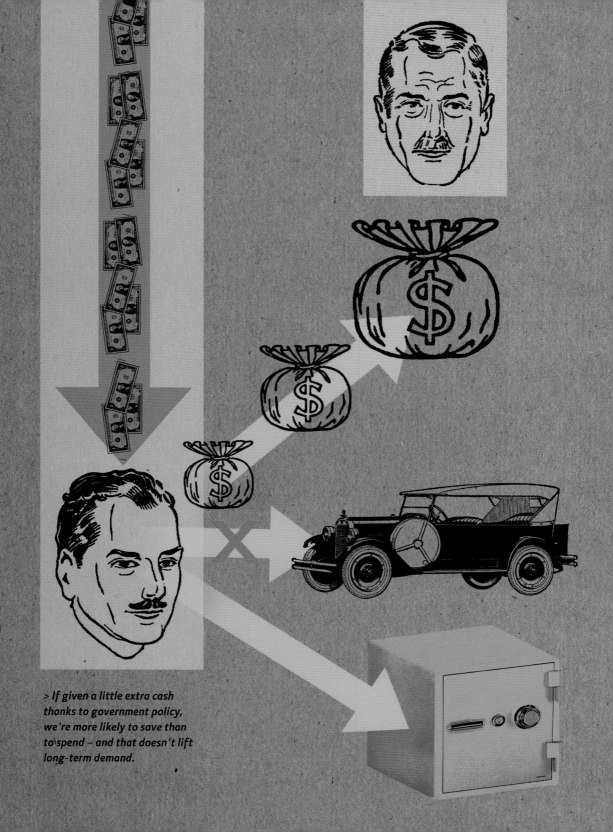

> If given a little extra cash thanks to government policy, we're more likely to save than to spend – and that doesn't lift long-term demand.

RATIONAL EXPECTATIONS

the 30-second theory

3-SECOND CRASH
You make decisions about the future on the basis of available information. Even if it turns out to be wrong, that was still the most rational decision to make.

3-MINUTE BOOM
The use of rational expectations theory to explain the stagflation of the 1970s makes sense only after you've proven that the Phillips curve does not work in the long run. But the theory assumes that this is something that firms and workers considered to be true all along. Wasn't it more the case that everyone realized it progressively during the 1970s? In that case, it is adaptive expectations (past information) that guided the behaviour of firms and workers and not rational expectations.

During the 1970s, when expansionary government policies could not reduce unemployment – although they increased inflation – a wave of free market economists adapted John Muth's theory of 'rational expectations' to explain why. The theory states that when workers and firms make decisions about the future, they base them on currently available information, rather than on past information (which was the assumption of economists up until then). This information includes what governments say they will do as well as what critics of the government say, such as the opposition parties or economic commentators. For example, if the government tries to boost the economy and reduce unemployment by expanding the money supply, firms and workers will consider not only the short-term lift to growth, but also the longer-term increase in inflation. Firms and labour unions will immediately seek price and wage rises because they expect inflation to rise. The result is that unemployment will not drop, even temporarily, while the long-term effect of expansionary policies – more inflation – will still happen. The impact of these ideas was such that many economists speak of the 'rational expectations revolution'. The two most famous rational expectations theorists are Robert Lucas and Thomas Sargent.

RELATED THEORIES
See also
THE PHILLIPS CURVE
page 52
TIME CONSISTENCY
page 58
PERMANENT INCOME
HYPOTHESIS
page 54
EFFICIENT MARKET
HYPOTHESIS
page 152

3-SECOND BIOGRAPHIES
JOHN MUTH
1930–2005

ROBERT LUCAS
1937–

THOMAS SARGENT
1943–

30-SECOND TEXT
Christakis Georgiou

'You can fool some of the people all of the time, and all of the people some of the time, but you cannot fool all of the people all of the time.'
ABRAHAM LINCOLN

> *People use all the information at their fingertips, including forecasts of the future, to make decisions. Policy makers should never assume that people can be persistently fooled.*

TIME CONSISTENCY

the 30-second theory

It sounds like a good idea for

policy makers to be able to respond to changing circumstances. But time consistency shows that if government makes a policy, it should stick to it. Why? Take an example from politics: negotiating over hostages. Most countries announce that they won't negotiate, because if there's no reward, rational terrorists won't bother taking hostages. But when a hostage is taken, governments are tempted to make a concession and bring the hostage home. The problem is, if terrorists expect government to change its tune, its 'no negotiations' announcement won't deter hostage-taking. The same story can play out in monetary policy, as shown by economists Edward Prescott and Finn Kydland. When the Federal Reserve announces low inflation is its main goal, firms and workers act accordingly and negotiate small wage increases. Later, though, the Fed may be tempted to use expansionary monetary policy – to cut interest rates and increase inflation – to reduce unemployment. It might work in the short term, but firms and workers learn to expect this inconsistency and negotiate for higher wages, which generates higher inflation without increasing employment. The solution, Prescott and Kydland argued, is rules instead of discretion.

3-SECOND CRASH
To achieve a policy you want, in the long run it's best to just stick to it.

3-MINUTE BOOM
The theory of time consistency has had wide-reaching effects. It's been used to explain the 'stagflation' of the 1970s: when decision makers' preferences changed over time, both inflation and unemployment rose while business activity stagnated. It's also used to make a case for the independence of central banks. If they're tied to political pressures or partisan government agendas, they may make short-term decisions that hurt the economy in the long term.

RELATED THEORIES
See also
RATIONAL EXPECTATIONS
page 56
RATIONAL CHOICE
page 106
PUBLIC CHOICE
page 112
EXPECTED UTILITY THEORY
page 114

3-SECOND BIOGRAPHIES
FINN KYDLAND
1943–
EDWARD PRESCOTT
1940–

30-SECOND TEXT
Katie Huston

'It seems likely that the current practice of selecting that policy which is best, given the current situation, is likely to converge to the consistent but suboptimal policy.'
KYDLAND AND PRESCOTT

> Once a government has decided on a course of action, it should maintain that course in order for goals to be achieved.

FINANCIAL ACCELERATOR

the 30-second theory

3-SECOND CRASH
Losses make it harder
to borrow, which in turn
leads to more losses; and
every time the problem
gets bigger. It's like a
financial snowball.

3-MINUTE BOOM
It's reasonable to assume
that an economy in a
strong financial position
will keep doing well, and
vice versa. But what
determines the initial
kickoff, virtuous or
vicious? If this is the
mechanism that
determines the health
of a firm or an economy,
we need to explain what
might push an economy
into a weak financial
situation in the first place.

What's the impact of a weak
financial system on the development of a
financial crisis? Current Federal Reserve chairman
Ben Bernanke started his career by theorizing
that such a situation would make a financial
crisis worse by accelerating its initial impact.
Imagine a firm that doesn't do as
well as it expected and thus finds itself with
fewer funds at its disposal. This means that
its creditworthiness gets worse and so it
becomes harder for it to raise outside capital
by borrowing. Now if the firm is a bank, and
worse still, if all the banks in an economy are
in the same situation, they can't fulfil the
role of financing the economy (giving loans
to corporations, credit to consumers, and so
on). So credit becomes a lot more expensive
and some firms go bankrupt because they can't
raise outside capital. In turn, this has an adverse
impact on the banks that had lent money to
these firms. The whole thing resembles a
rolling snowball getting bigger and bigger
and accelerating the financial crisis. Something
like this happened during the recent 'subprime'
crisis, when weakened banks had to take huge
losses from their mortgage operations and then
stopped lending to each other, so leading to the
credit crunch.

RELATED THEORIES
See also
LENDER OF LAST RESORT
page 64
KEYNESIAN ECONOMICS
(POSITIVE)
page 16

3-SECOND BIOGRAPHIES
BEN BERNANKE
1953–

MARK GERTLER
1951–

30-SECOND TEXT
Christakis Georgiou

'Just as a healthy
financial system
promotes growth,
adverse financial
conditions may
prevent an economy
from reaching
its potential.'

BEN BERNANKE

> *A strong economy can keep growing stronger, but a weak one, thanks to self-perpetuating financial circumstances, will keep getting weaker.*

FINANCIAL INSTABILITY HYPOTHESIS

the 30-second theory

3-SECOND CRASH
Stability makes people reckless. Borrowers borrow to excess; lenders lend to excess. And then the resulting defaults cause a financial crisis.

3-MINUTE BOOM
Minsky's theory seems to fit the financial crisis of the late 2000s particularly well. Consumers saw house prices rising year after year, and thus became more aggressive in taking out loans that could only be paid off by house price appreciation. Lenders became more aggressive in offering risky loans – not only 'subprime' mortgages, but also loans to other firms. When people started to default on their payments, then the loans were transformed from a profit machine into a death warrant for those who had issued them.

The recent financial crisis has been a marvel for the posthumous reputation of Hyman Minsky, an economist who remained in the fringes during his lifetime. Minsky said that financial crises are endemic in capitalism. They arise because in times of prolonged prosperity, borrowers tend to become less careful when borrowing and lenders more reckless when lending. Because of that, speculative bubbles arise in the financial system. Whereas before, most borrowers were 'hedge borrowers' – that is, they could repay the principal and the interest on their loan from the profits they made – progressively more and more borrowers become 'speculative' or 'Ponzi' borrowers – that is, they can only repay out of their profits the interest on their loan or not even that, in which case they have to sell their own assets to raise money to repay their debt. The problem is that this can drag the whole system down. When 'speculative' and 'Ponzi' borrowers emerge, the amount of debt in the system soars until it becomes obvious that it cannot be repaid and that someone has to pay the price of this systemic insolvency. 'Speculative' and 'Ponzi' borrowers then default, lenders tighten the grip on credit, and that drives the economy into recession.

RELATED THEORIES
See also
MORAL HAZARD
page 150
FINANCIAL ACCELERATOR
page 60

3-SECOND BIOGRAPHIES
HYMAN MINSKY
1919–1996
CHARLES KINDLEBERGER
1910–2003

30-SECOND TEXT
Christakis Georgiou

'Stability is unstable.'
HYMAN MINSKY

> *Prolonged periods of growth can lead to recklessness – and when the bubble bursts …*

LENDER OF
LAST RESORT

the 30-second theory

The lender of last resort is an institution that provides emergency funds to other financial institutions at a time of stress or crisis. Such a role is usually played by a national central bank, which provides what have recently become popularly known as 'bail out' loans in order to ensure important financial institutions do not collapse. The existence of a lender of last resort provides a safety net to banks and other lending institutions in the form of government-backed loans. These loans, however, are not unconditional. They require the recipient to maintain sufficient collateral – in the form of financial assets and so on – and to pay penalty interest rates. For example, if you run out of petrol on the motorway, you must not only pay to refill it, but also the additional 'penalty' cost of having a tow truck come to rescue you. Loans made by the International Monetary Fund (IMF) to countries with serious financial imbalances are also classified as fulfilling the lender of last resort function. Such loans are usually provided to developing countries to address chronic balance-of-payments problems and instabilities in their financial markets. Extensive conditions are attached to these loans, outlining strict repayment terms and reforms to market regulation.

3-SECOND CRASH
A safety net for financial crises – protecting the public interest?

3-MINUTE BOOM
The most common criticism regarding the lender of last resort is that it encourages excessive risk taking by financial institutions and governments. If a safety net is provided, economic actors are more likely to take potentially dangerous risks. Yet when such risk taking undermines deposit-holding banks and developing country governments, they are likely to significantly affect those people that depend upon them. Thus to protect these individuals, is the lender of last resort a necessity?

RELATED THEORY
See also
MORAL HAZARD
page 150

3-SECOND BIOGRAPHIES
WALTER BAGEHOT
1826–1877

CHARLES GOODHART
1936–

GARY GORTON
1951–

BEN BERNANKE
1953–

CHARLES CALOMIRIS
1957–

30-SECOND TEXT
Adam Fishwick

'Lend freely at a high rate, on good collateral.'
WALTER BAGEHOT

> By providing financial bailout, the lender of last resort aims to ease financial pressure – but at a cost.

GROWTH

GROWTH
GLOSSARY

capitalism An economic system whereby the means of production (factories and so forth) and distribution are owned primarily by private individuals or corporations. The prices of labour and goods are determined on the free market, and not by central government. Profits are claimed by individual company owners or, in the case of most corporations, distributed to shareholders.

convergence hypothesis The idea that slow-developing economies will eventually catch up (or nearly catch up) with fast-developing ones. This is based on the theory of diminishing returns, whereby the bigger the economy, the slower it grows; whereas a smaller economy has a much greater capacity for growth.

diminishing returns The concept that beyond a certain point of optimal efficiency industrial production becomes increasingly inefficient.

endogenous growth An alternative to the neoclassical/exogenous growth theory, it attempts to explain how technological improvements take place. This model puts great emphasis on innovation and entrepreneurship and on the development of human capital (that is the development of a skilled labour force). It also shows how government policies, including subsidies for research and development, can influence growth.

exogenous growth The neoclassical growth theory developed by Robert Solow and Trevor W. Swan in the 1950s. It aims to show how technology, capital, and the size of the labour force combine to create growth. Crucially, though, it fails to explain how improvement in technology (that is, innovation) occurs.

green technology The use of technology to minimize human impact on the environment. This is done mainly through increased efficiency, reduced pollution, and the use of alternative sources of energy. Typical applications of green technology include: recycling, renewable energy, water purification, waste reduction, and sewage treatment.

gross domestic product (GDP) The sum of all goods and services sold in a country during a given year. The most common formula for calculating this is: consumption + investment + government spending + (exports – imports). GDP is commonly used as a shorthand to measure a country's economic performance – the assumption being that a high GDP indicates a successful economy.
This approach has come under criticism as being too narrow an indicator of success, ignoring as it does other important quality-of-life factors, such as wealth distribution, life expectancy, and environmental degradation.

infrastructure The basic structures that enable and facilitate modern societies to function. These include roads, railways, water supplies, sewers, power supplies, schools, and hospitals. As well as making human life more comfortable, they also enable businesses to operate efficiently, for example by providing the means by which goods and raw materials are transported.

monopoly The dominance of a market by one firm to the exclusion of all others.

steady-state economy An economy that has reached an optimum size, in which, however, innovation can still occur, leading to growth. This type of economy is usually linked to a static population size and reduced consumption. In environmental terms, a steady-state economy is one that is kept within its natural ecological constraints.

sustainable Managing resources within the capacity of the planet to replenish them.

NEOCLASSICAL GROWTH

the 30-second theory

3-SECOND CRASH
Growth depends on three things: technological change, capital accumulation and the growth of the labour force.

3-MINUTE BOOM
In the neoclassical growth model, technological change is a key factor in growth, but it is external, or exogenous: the model doesn't address where technological change comes from, how it happens, or why it might differ across countries. Critics also point out that the theory doesn't take entrepreneurship, human capital, competition, or the quality of government policies into account – factors that have also been shown to influence economic development.

Neoclassical growth theory aims to predict a country's long-term economic development. Known as the Solow-Swan model (after the economists who developed it in 1956), the theory focuses on how three factors – technology, capital and the size of the labour force – drive economic growth. Increasing capital creates growth because people can be more productive with more capital – up to a point. However, the theory incorporates the idea of diminishing returns. When a company has one worker and adds one more, output increases dramatically. But when you have one hundred workers and add one more, output might not rise that much and, at a certain point, it stops increasing unless technology changes. Eventually, countries achieve a steady-state economy, where GDP (gross domestic product) grows slowly – at the same rate as the labour force plus technological progress. Neoclassical growth theory also predicts that the gap between poor and rich countries will narrow – the so-called convergence hypothesis. Because poor countries have less capital to start with, each additional unit of capital produces higher returns than it would in a capital-rich country. But while countries with similar economies, infrastructures and institutions may converge (such as European Union countries), poor countries won't catch up entirely, but will reach their own level of steady-state economy.

RELATED THEORIES
See also
NEW GROWTH THEORY
page 72
CREATIVE DESTRUCTION
page 76
HUMAN CAPITAL
page 78
LIMITS TO GROWTH
page 82

3-SECOND BIOGRAPHIES
ROBERT SOLOW
1924–
TREVOR W. SWAN
1918–1989

30-SECOND TEXT
Katie Huston

'There is no evidence that God ever intended the United States of America to have a higher per capita income than the rest of the world for eternity.'
ROBERT SOLOW

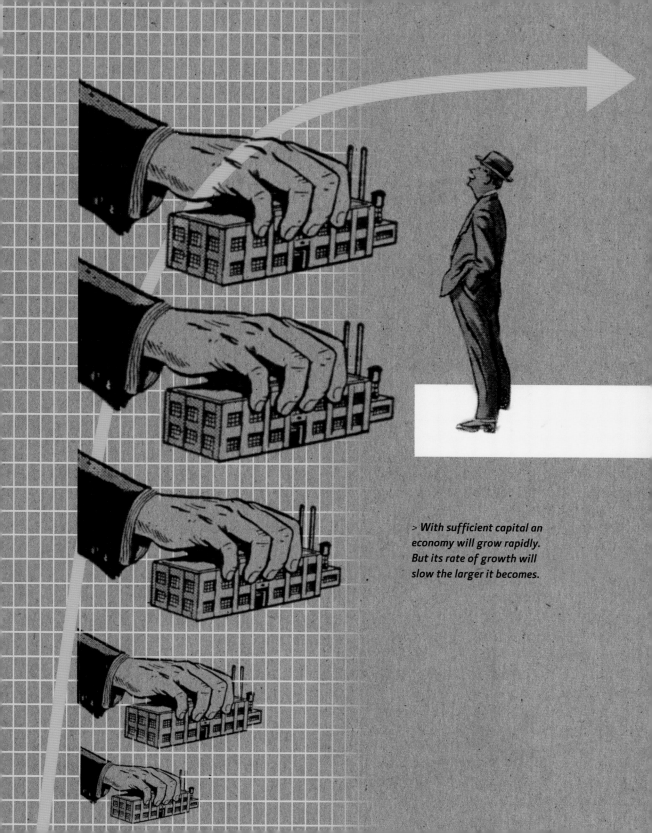

> With sufficient capital an economy will grow rapidly. But its rate of growth will slow the larger it becomes.

NEW GROWTH THEORY

the 30-second theory

3-SECOND CRASH
Capital and labour are nice, but economic growth is all about innovation.

3-MINUTE BOOM
New growth theory implies that governments should invest in promoting investment in innovation. They should provide an environment within which this will occur by constructing a well-designed intellectual property rights system, for example. Yet how can the governments of developing countries overcome the barriers that limit their ability to pursue such policies? Low levels of infrastructural and administrative development, limited tax revenues, and endemic problems of corruption mean that this remains particularly difficult.

New, or 'endogenous', growth theory emerged from a dissatisfaction with neoclassical explanations. The neoclassical model attributed economic growth to the accumulation of capital, a growing labour force, and an externally-driven process of technological change. But economists began to ask where technological change comes from. New ideas don't simply drop from heaven, they are the result of hard work and investment. Researchers invest their time trying to understand how the world works, major companies work constantly to improve their products, and entrepreneurs tinker in their garages to build better widgets. Such investment in innovation is a key factor that explains how growth rates differ across countries. Innovation often produces benefits that go beyond a single firm or entrepreneur. For example, a high-technology manufacturer will bring new ideas to an area in which they invest. Public investment in education, infrastructure, and research and development then support the dissemination of these within the economy. Resulting innovations will, in turn, enhance the technology and skills base of the economy. Endogenous (developing from within) growth theory recognizes that these originate from economic agents within an economy – hence the term 'endogenous growth'.

RELATED THEORIES
See also
NEOCLASSICAL GROWTH
page 70
HUMAN CAPITAL
page 78

3-SECOND BIOGRAPHY
PAUL ROMER
1955–

30-SECOND TEXT
Adam Fishwick

'Economic growth occurs whenever people take resources and rearrange them in ways that make them more valuable ... human history teaches us, however, that economic growth springs from better recipes, not just more cooking.'
PAUL ROMER

> *Innovation is a direct cause of healthy growth, but innovation doesn't happen by accident – it needs investment.*

1766
Born, Surrey, England

1784
Enters Jesus College, Cambridge

1797
Ordained minister of Church of England

1798
Publishes *An Essay on the Principle of Population*

1804
Marries cousin Harriet

1805
Appointed Professor of History and Political Economy at Haileybury College, Hertfordshire

1815
Publishes *The Nature of Rent*

1820
Publishes *Principles of Political Economy*

1827
Publishes *Definitions in Political Economy*

1834
Dies, Bath, England

THOMAS MALTHUS

Mere mention of the word

'eugenics' nowadays is likely to be met with a snort of derision, soon followed by a reference to the Nazis. The response was much the same when Thomas Malthus raised the subject back in 1798. In *An Essay on the Principle of Population*, Malthus, an Anglican priest, suggested that the population of the world would grow so much that it would eventually outstrip the resources required to sustain it. His solutions included doing away with the Poor Laws, which he said encouraged the poor to remain poor and to breed more poor, and instead to allow them to meet their end and, therefore, prevent future suffering. His ideas invited the scorn of most of his contemporaries, including the poet Shelley, who described him as 'a eunuch and a tyrant', and later writers, such as Marx, who said he was 'the principal enemy of the people'.

Yet, to those who knew Thomas Malthus personally, he was a tall, handsome, gentle fellow, with a cleft palate that made his speech hard to follow – although his writing was suffused with energy.

Brought up on a country estate in Surrey, Malthus studied at Jesus College, Cambridge, and was ordained a minister of the Church of England in 1788. His father was personal friends with David Hume and Jean-Jacques Rousseau and encouraged his son's discursive streak. In 1805, Malthus became Professor of History and Political Economy at Haileybury College in Hertfordshire, where he trained employees of the East India Company to become efficient administrators. In return, his students referred to him as 'Pop' (as in 'Population') Malthus. Despite the comments of his detractors, he was happily married, with three children.

Although Malthus' ideas incurred the fury of his contemporaries, he also had some notable followers. Charles Darwin credited him as an important influence, and John Maynard Keynes was also an admirer. With the growing emphasis on economic sustainability, population growth is once again on the agenda, and Malthus' ideas are gaining currency. The bad boy of economics may yet have the last laugh.

CREATIVE DESTRUCTION

the 30-second theory

3-SECOND CRASH
In with the new, out
with the old – it's how
our economy grows.

3-MINUTE BOOM
According to creative
destruction, companies
should fail when someone
better comes along – the
government shouldn't
help Polaroid when digital
takes over, nor protect
small businesses when
massive corporates come
to town. But what about
bailing out the banks and
car companies? When the
banks go bust, the whole
economy takes a hit, and
unemployed factory
workers can't afford
haircuts or holidays, so
hairdressers and travel
agents close, too. Can a
company or bank be 'too
big to fail'?

New products are always killing old ones. Think of Polaroid®: the company had a monopoly on instant photography until the digital camera came along. Suddenly, Polaroid's profits fell because other companies were making cheaper alternatives. Or take DVDs: now they're on the scene, videotapes are worth pennies. No one makes them anymore, and companies that did have been forced to produce something new in order to stay alive. Joseph Schumpeter called this process creative destruction – when a company creates a new product, improves technology, discovers a better supply source, pioneers a more efficient way to produce, or finds a better method of industrial organization, it can destroy its competition. Unlike traditional economics, which focuses on price competition, this theory focuses on competition from new products or technologies. Creative destruction is driven by entrepreneurs who put new ideas into action. Schumpeter argued that this innovation is the driving force behind long-term economic growth, and called creative destruction 'the essential fact about capitalism'. Ruined companies and disappearing industries are all part of the bigger picture, which is painful, but inevitable – even necessary – as new companies emerge and new jobs get created, setting the stage for economies to grow.

RELATED THEORIES
See also
AUSTRIAN SCHOOL
page 22
NEW GROWTH THEORY
page 72

3-SECOND BIOGRAPHY
JOSEPH SCHUMPETER
1883–1950

30-SECOND TEXT
Katie Huston

'The fundamental impulse that sets and keeps the capitalist engine in motion comes from the new consumers, goods, the new methods of production or transportation, the new markets, the new forms of industrial organization that capitalist enterprise creates.'
JOSEPH SCHUMPETER

> *Technological advances and innovative production methods are just two forces of change that see some companies rise and others fall.*

HUMAN CAPITAL

the 30-second theory

On average, people with university degrees make more money than people without them. That's because education, like job training, creates more human capital – knowledge, skills, expertise and health – which creates both personal economic gain and general economic development. Adam Smith recognized that people contribute to economic growth, not just machines and money. In the 1950s and 1960s, economist Jacob Mincer used human capital theory to explain differences in personal incomes, and showed that annual earnings rose 5 to 10 per cent for every year of additional schooling. As Gary Becker argued in the 1960s, paying for education, training and health is a rational economic choice. Healthy, educated and skilled workers are more productive, efficient and innovative, which bolsters the economy. What's more, human capital (unlike land or machinery) is self-generating, transportable and shareable. The more a doctor works, the more knowledge and skill he gains, and if he teaches others, he still possesses and uses that knowledge. However, some knowledge is more transferable than others; specific human capital, such as a particular task on an assembly line, is useful in only one company or industry, while general human capital, such as literacy or computer programming, is more widely valuable.

RELATED THEORIES
See also
CREATIVE DESTRUCTION
page 76
RATIONAL CHOICE
page 106

3-SECOND BIOGRAPHIES
ADAM SMITH
1723–1790

GARY BECKER
1930–

JACOB MINCER
1922–2006

30-SECOND TEXT
Katie Huston

3-SECOND CRASH
Investing isn't just for machines and factories. When you invest in people, you get more in return.

3-MINUTE BOOM
Human capital can help explain why countries develop – or don't. After the Second World War, Europe's economy sprang back to life quite quickly, even though its factories and infrastructure were largely destroyed, thanks to its human capital. But countries in which human capital is sparse, particularly those with low literacy rates, struggle to develop, especially when the most educated or skilled people move overseas to earn higher returns on their human capital – an effect known as the 'brain drain'.

'More highly educated and skilled persons almost always tend to earn more than others.'
GARY BECKER

> *Increasing human capital by investing in training and education creates wealthier individuals and a wealthier economy.*

THE RULE OF LAW

the 30-second theory

3-SECOND CRASH
No one should be above the law – not even the government – and courts should be totally independent.

3-MINUTE BOOM
The rule of law is deemed so important for a free market economy that in the early 1990s the IMF and the World Bank began conditioning financial assistance on the implementation of the rule of law in recipient countries. Because of this, many critics say that the rule of law is a form of subtle blackmail by the West in order to gain access to the economies of developing nations.

Free markets supposedly work wonders. But for that to happen you need more than a buyer and a seller, or rather you need someone or something to arbitrate between the two in case they get into a fight. After the fall of the Soviet Union, and when its former countries' economies started liberalizing, many economists pointed out that for solid growth to take place through the free market, the rule of law had to be restored or introduced in those countries. This means the existence of well-documented and clear laws, of an independent judiciary capable of enforcing them, and the submission of government officials to those laws. This is important because in the free market every transaction is done on the basis of a contract – whether between two multinationals or when buying a beer at a bar – and if this contract is breached, then someone should be able to impose its correct implementation. The rule of law is essential if you want to attract foreign investors. They must be reassured that their investments will not be abused and that they will be able to have recourse to impartial courts if necessary.

RELATED THEORY
See also
FREE MARKET CAPITALISM
page 28

3-SECOND BIOGRAPHIES
HERNANDO DE SOTO
1941–

DOUGLAS NORTH
1920–

30-SECOND TEXT
Christakis Georgiou

'The "something momentous" was that Americans and Europeans were on the verge of establishing widespread formal property law and inventing the conversion process in that law that allowed them to create capital. This was the moment when the West crossed the demarcation line that led to successful capitalism.'

HERNANDO DE SOTO

> The rule of law helps to ensure that if a contract is signed, deals must be adhered to. So you want to buy a factory?

LIMITS TO GROWTH

the 30-second theory

In 1798, Thomas Malthus pointed out that if the world population kept growing, people would die. Why? Because of resource scarcity. Malthus noted that population increases exponentially or 'geometrically' (the more people there are, the more people they can make), while food follows linear or 'arithmetic' growth (because the earth has limited resources). Think of it this way: in geometric growth the population doubles every 25 years: 100, 200, 400, 800 ... But in arithmetic growth, the amount of food only increases enough to feed 100 more people every 25 years: 100, 200, 300, 400. Malthus predicted that continued population growth would lead to widespread disease, famine and death. His warnings didn't prove true, fortunately, but his basic ideas were revived in the 1970s, when a group of scientists, economists, businessmen and politicians raised concerns about the limits to growth. The gist? The economy can't keep on pursuing growth, because our planet can only support a limited population. Famine is a risk, but even if that doesn't kill us, we will eventually run out of resources, such as oil, copper, trees and fish – not to mention the risk of pollution. The 'limits to growth' view warns that humans must reduce their environmental footprint and population growth, or suffer dire consequences of resource scarcity, famine and climate change.

RELATED THEORIES
See also
THE TRAGEDY OF THE COMMONS
page 142
POLLUTER PAYS PRINCIPLE
page 146

3-SECOND CRASH
The economy can't keep on growing forever, because there's not enough to go around.

3-MINUTE BOOM
Most economists believe the market can solve resource scarcity; for example, when oil's running low, prices rise, encouraging people to consume less and find new oil sources. But this process doesn't always work, especially for environmental goods, such as fisheries, which lack strong property rights. In such cases, government may have to make growth sustainable by moderating it with economic incentives, such as high pollution taxes or funding green technology. The most radical argue that economics' goal of long-term growth is inherently unsustainable, and call for 'degrowth' – consuming less.

3-SECOND BIOGRAPHY
THOMAS MALTHUS
1766–1834

30-SECOND AUTHOR
Katie Huston

'The power of population is indefinitely greater than the power in the earth to produce subsistence for man.'
THOMAS MALTHUS

> *The human population, and by extension the global consumer economy, cannot continue to grow indefinitely – eventually there'll be nothing left to consume.*

100 200 400 800 160

100 200 300 400 500

GLOBAL TRADE

Big Mac Index A theory devised by *The Economist* magazine to illustrate the real value of currencies. The idea is that a Big Mac produced in the United States should have the same relative value as a Big Mac produced in Pakistan. By comparing the price of Big Macs in those two countries, you establish a Big Mac exchange rate. You then compare that to the actual exchange rate of the countries' currencies. If the currency exchange rate is greater than the Big Mac rate, it suggests the currency is overvalued; if it's lower, then the currency is undervalued.

capital mobility The ability of money to be exchanged across national boundaries. In earlier times, this was often restricted by governments to bolster their currency. With the advent of globalization, restrictions are now minimal.

exchange rate The value of one currency relative to another. For instance, US$1 may be worth £0.61; in which case £1 is worth US$1.63. In earlier times, exchange rates were often fixed (or 'pegged'); nowadays they are mostly unfixed and determined by the markets.

free trade The unrestricted exchange of goods between countries without government intervention. In practice, most governments influence trade in various ways, either by subsidizing their own products (for example, through measures such as the EU agricultural policy), or imposing tariffs and/or quotas on imported goods (the Smoot-Hawley Tariff imposed in the United States in the 1930s being one example).

labour mobility The ability of workers to move around a country and between countries. Greater labour mobility benefits industry because it increases the pool of labour available; it benefits workers because it allows them to improve their opportunities. Conversely, it can also threaten resident workers' status, because migrant workers compete with them for jobs.

macroeconomics The study of the whole economy (from 'macro', meaning 'big'). Typically, macroeconomics attempts to explain the relationships between GDP, unemployment, inflation, interest rates, trade, and other economic factors. This contrasts with microeconomics, which looks at actions of companies and individuals and how they affect particular markets.

monetarism A school of thought, headed by economist Milton Friedman, which asserts that the supply of money is the most important factor in a country's economic performance. Too much money in the economy leads to high inflation, so the supply of money needs to be tightly controlled. On the other hand, too little money in the economy leads to higher interest rates, which means that consumers are tempted to save more and spend less.

monopoly The dominance of a market by one firm to the exclusion of all others.

oligopoly The dominance of a market by a few firms, to the exclusion of most others (from the Greek *oligos*, meaning 'a few', and *polein*, meaning 'to sell'). Although not as potentially damaging as a monopoly, this situation may lead to collusion and price-fixing between companies.

subsidies Payments, usually from central government, designed to support producers or manufacturers in strategically important industries. Reasons for granting subsidies vary from maintaining a source of employment to wanting to remain self-sufficient in food or other produce. Subsidies may also be used to protect local products from cheap overseas imports and thereby improve a country's balance of payments.

tariff A tax imposed on goods being transported from one country to another. The idea of imposing tariffs is usually to inflate the price of imported products to make locally-produced products more attractive. This is a form of protectionism. Trade blocks, such as the EU, are formed to eradicate tariffs and allow free trade between member nations – although nonmember nations may still be subject to tariffs and find it even more difficult to trade with members of such a block. In less-developed countries, tariffs may also be an important source of government revenue.

COMPARATIVE ADVANTAGE

the 30-second theory

RELATED THEORY
See also
FREE MARKET CAPITALISM
page 28

3-SECOND BIOGRAPHY
DAVID RICARDO
(1772–1823)

30-SECOND TEXT
Katie Huston

3-SECOND CRASH
You produce what you're 'most best' at, and I'll make what I'm 'least worst' at – there'll be more for everyone.

3-MINUTE BOOM
Ricardo's theory is still the best way to explain trade's benefits, but it has limits. The simple theory glosses over some real-world complications, such as transport costs, unemployment, the cost of moving labour or capital from one industry to another, trade barriers, such as subsidies and tariffs, and differentiation among products – factors that can be important. Ricardo also assumed that capital couldn't move across borders, which has brought his theory under heavy fire in the age of international capital mobility and transnational corporations.

Kate and Sawyer are stuck on a deserted island. Kate can catch ten fish or gather ten mangoes per day; Sawyer can get four fish or eight mangoes. If they fend for themselves, and split their time equally, Kate will have five fish and five mangoes per day; Sawyer, two fish and four mangoes – seven fish and nine mangoes in all. Kate has an absolute advantage in both foods, but that doesn't mean that she should both catch fish and gather mangoes. If they decide to trade, they can both eat more than they would get if each tried to do both activities. How? It's all about opportunity cost – how many fish they have to give up per mango, and vice versa. To catch a fish, Kate forfeits one mango, while Sawyer loses two, so Kate has a lower opportunity cost, and thus a comparative advantage in fish. However, Sawyer has the comparative advantage in mangoes; he loses half a fish per mango, while Kate loses a whole fish. If they specialize, Kate can catch ten fish, and Sawyer can gather eight mangoes. Or Kate can catch nine fish and gather one mango, for nine fish and nine mangoes in all – two more fish than they started with. Ricardo applied this theory to international trade: if countries specialize according to their comparative advantage and trade freely, everyone will be better off.

'If two countries can both of them produce two commodities, corn, for example, and cloth, but not both commodities, with the same comparative facility, the two countries will find their advantage in confining themselves, each to one of the commodities, bartering for the other.'

JAMES MILL

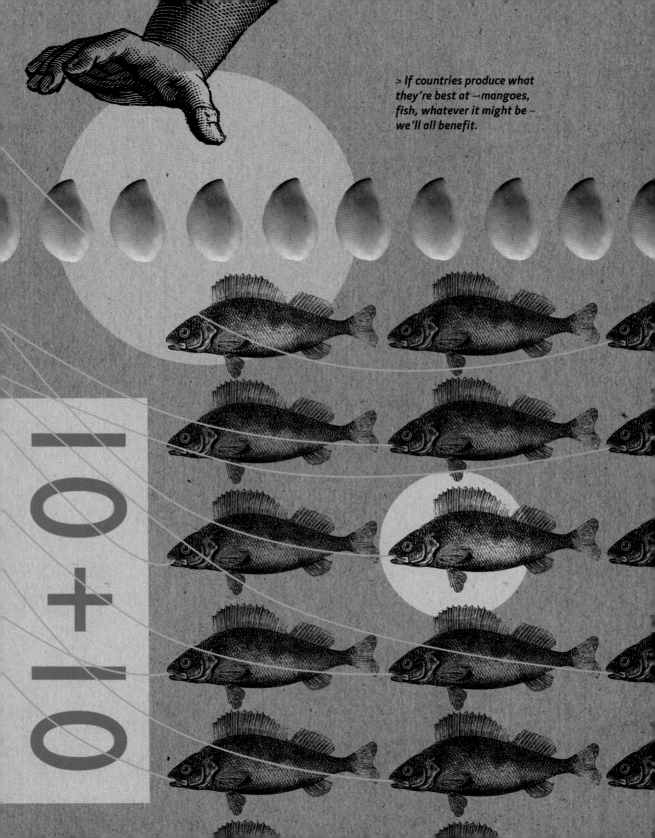

> If countries produce what they're best at — mangoes, fish, whatever it might be — we'll all benefit.

HECKSCHER-OHLIN TRADE MODEL
the 30-second theory

3-SECOND CRASH
It's not who you are but what you've got – that's what makes comparative advantage!

3-MINUTE BOOM
The Heckscher-Ohlin trade model predicts that capital-abundant countries will export capital-intensive products and leave labour-intensive production to countries with an abundance of cheap labour. Yet this implies that the latter will continue to export lower-value goods in exchange for the high-technology goods of the former. Such patterns are arguably historically constructed, but what role has government played? Has it passively supported comparative advantage, or has it actively sought to create it?

Building on the theory of

comparative advantage, Eli Heckscher and Bertil Ohlin argued that permanent but different labour productivity across countries was insufficient for explaining the benefits from free trade. Instead, they sought to extend this theory by taking into account the varying factors of production – land, labour, and capital – and how these determined comparative advantage. For example, while a developed country, such as the United States, has a relative abundance of capital and skilled labour, a developing country, such as Mexico, has a relative abundance of less-skilled labour. Therefore, for each country to benefit from free trade they should concentrate on those types of production that utilize their comparatively cheapest factors. Capital-and-skills-intensive production, such as software, pharmaceuticals, and aircraft will thus occur in the United States, while labour-intensive production, such as raw materials or product assembly, will take place in Mexico. Such specialization increases the benefits of trade. For example, developed countries can purchase lower-cost products and raw materials on the international market, while developing countries have access to cheaper technology imports. Growth will be boosted by such imports, whilst the concentration upon labour-intensive production will see wage rates rise in response to the raised demand for labour.

RELATED THEORIES
See also
NEOCLASSICAL GROWTH
page 70
NEW TRADE THEORY
page 92

3-SECOND BIOGRAPHIES
ELI HECKSCHER
1879–1952

BERTIL OHLIN
1899–1979

PAUL SAMUELSON
1915–

30-SECOND TEXT
Adam Fishwick

'Commodities requiring for their production much of the [relatively abundant factors of production] and little of the [relatively scarce factors] are exported in exchange for goods that call for factors in the opposite proportions.'

BERTIL OHLIN

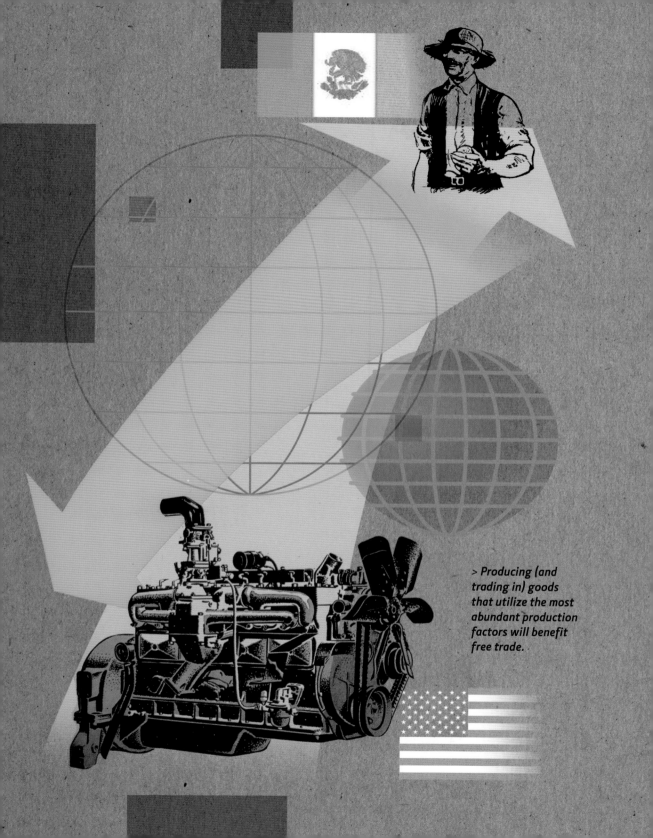

> Producing (and trading in) goods that utilize the most abundant production factors will benefit free trade.

NEW TRADE THEORY

the 30-second theory

3-SECOND CRASH
If bigger firms are more efficient, then maybe governments can help create competitive advantage.

3-MINUTE BOOM
The Japanese success in exporting more advanced industrial products is claimed to provide strong evidence for the continued significance of industrial policy for international trade. Yet the monopolies that such policy contributes to can prevent necessary structural changes and give too much influence to such government-backed firms. Moreover, are governments always the best judges of investment decisions? They can often make mistakes, and these must be balanced against the alleged benefits of such intervention.

Writing during the 1960s and 1970s, 'new trade theorist' Paul Krugman sought to highlight two neglected elements of international trade: increasing returns to scale and imperfect competition. By concentrating on the nature of industrial production, he argued that 'economies of scale' provide large firms with a considerable advantage in that they are able to produce at a far lower cost than smaller new firms entering into a particular industry. This implies that being an early entrant into an industry can give firms a big advantage in accruing increasing returns and crowding out potential competitors. An important result of this is a situation of monopolistic or oligopolistic competition, whereby large firms located in capital-rich countries dominate particular industries and shape the profile of international trade. New trade theorists argued that government intervention might be able to recreate such a situation. Protective tariffs and subsidies could allow particular firms to flourish and thus 'create' a competitive advantage that was not already in existence. If a school football team is given access to the best coaches, the best training facilities, and plays regularly against the best teams, it is likely to become the best – government support for firms should act in much the same way.

RELATED THEORIES
See also
FREE MARKET CAPITALISM
page 28
MERCANTILISM
page 36
NEW GROWTH THEORY
page 72
COMPARATIVE ADVANTAGE
page 88
RENT SEEKING
page 154

3-SECOND BIOGRAPHIES
ELHANAN HELPMAN
1946–
PAUL KRUGMAN
1953–

30-SECOND TEXT
Adam Fishwick

'A small "head-start" for one region will cumulate over time, with exports of manufactures from the leading region crowding out the industrial sector of the lagging region.'
PAUL KRUGMAN

> If bigger is better, then governments should intervene to create bigger companies.

1772
Born, London

1786
Joins father's business

1793
Marries Priscilla Anne
Wilkinson

1810
Publishes *The High Price
of Bullion, a Proof of the
Depreciation of Bank
Notes*

1814
Retires a wealthy man

1815
Publishes *Essay on the
Influence of a Low Price
of Corn on the Profits of
Stock*

1817
Publishes *Principles of
Political Economy and
Taxation*

1819
Elected MP for
Portarlington, Ireland

1823
Dies, Gatcombe Park,
Gloucestershire

DAVID RICARDO

If a person is judged by their
actions, then certainly David Ricardo's
credentials in the world of finance are
recommendation enough for his more
philosophical ideas about economics. One of
seventeen children born to a Sephardic Jewish
family that emigrated from Holland to England
shortly before he was born, Ricardo inherited his
father's magic touch in the stock market. Joining
his father's business at the age of fourteen, he
quickly built up such a reputation that, when he
split with the family seven years later, he was
able to set up in business on his own. The reason
for the split? The level-headed stock broker fell
for a pretty Quaker girl and gave up his religion
and his family to marry her. His mother
apparently never spoke to him again. His success
in the stock market continued, however, so that
he was financially independent by the time he
was twenty-six and able to retire with a fortune
worth up to US$2.5 million by the time he was

forty-two. Along the way, he also fathered
eight children.

Ricardo was turned onto economics after
reading Adam Smith's *Wealth of Nations* in
his late twenties. He then adopted the subject
almost as a hobby, befriending some of the
great thinkers of the day, such as James Mill
and Thomas Malthus. Ricardo was an early
proponent of monetary theory, and caused a stir
in 1809 when he blamed the Bank of England for
creating inflation by printing too many bank
notes. His biggest contributions to economic
theory, however, were the law of diminishing
marginal returns – described in his essay *The
Influence of a Low Price of Corn on the Profits
of Stock* (1815 – and the theory of comparative
advantage, expounded in his definitive work
Principles of Political Economy and Taxation
of 1817. A Member of Parliament from 1819 until
his death in 1823, he was respected on both
sides of the political divide.

OPTIMUM CURRENCY AREA

the 30-second theory

How do you know whether a regional economy, such as a country, needs to have a single currency, or whether two or more countries should adopt the same currency? The economist Robert Mundell was awarded the Nobel Prize for Economics in 1999 for coming up with a theory that addressed this question. He said that if a number of regional economies do not respond in the same way to external shocks, then they should each have their own currency and adopt floating exchange rates. These could act as a buffer and help keep the various regional economies stable. How do we know whether there is sufficient homogeneity for a common currency though? Mundell proposed four criteria: workers must be ready to move across the region in search of jobs; there should be freedom of movement of capital; the economy should be diversified; and there should be a fiscal system that transfers money from one region to another when it is needed. The theory of the Optimum Currency Area was used to argue in favour of the creation of the euro, the common currency shared by sixteen European countries.

RELATED THEORY
See also
THE IMPOSSIBLE TRINITY
page 98

3-SECOND BIOGRAPHY
ROBERT MUNDELL
1932–

30-SECOND TEXT
Christakis Georgiou

3-SECOND CRASH
If an economy is homogeneous, then let it have a single currency. If not, each region should have a shared currency.

3-MINUTE BOOM
The problem with this theory is that it can only tell you whether an existing currency passes the test of the Optimum Currency Area or whether existing currencies can be merged into a new one. There is very little in the theory on how to move towards an Optimum Currency Area. A further difficulty is that the European Union does not fulfil all the criteria. It has very low labour mobility and no fiscal mechanism for transferring money from rich to poor regions.

'The advent of the euro may turn out to be the most important development in international monetary arrangements since the emergence of the dollar as the dominant currency shortly after the creation of the US central bank, the Federal Reserve System, in 1913.'

ROBERT MUNDELL

> At present there are sixteen countries in Europe whose economies are considered sufficiently homogenous to share a currency – the euro.

THE IMPOSSIBLE TRINITY

the 30-second theory

3-SECOND CRASH
Fixed exchange rate, international capital mobility, or control of monetary policy? Pick two, because you can't have it all. What a trilemma!

3-MINUTE BOOM
Capital mobility wasn't always a given; in fact, the history of the international monetary system boils down to which two goals governments pursue. Before the Great Depression, nations mostly chose capital mobility and fixed exchange rates, so their central banks couldn't combat unemployment. After the Second World War, countries implemented capital controls in order to have fixed exchange rates and control of monetary policy. But today, capital mobility isn't really optional – even China is lifting capital controls.

When it comes to monetary policy, countries want a lot of things. They may want a fixed exchange rate – where a currency's value is pegged to other currencies – to stabilize international trade. They want international capital mobility, so investors can move money in and out of the country. And they want control of domestic monetary policy, so they can change interest rates to combat unemployment or inflation. But Robert Mundell and Marcus Fleming proved in 1962 that you can only have two of the above – a principle also known as the 'trilemma'. Imagine Mexico chooses a fixed exchange rate. It also has capital mobility, because today international finance moves freely across borders, whether Mexico likes it or not. But if it tries to take control of monetary policy – for example, by cutting interest rates to combat unemployment – it has a problem. If interest rates fall, investors will flee from the currency to find higher yields elsewhere. That means Mexico has to defend the currency – using up precious reserves – or admit defeat and raise interest rates again. In short, if Mexico wants a fixed exchange rate and capital mobility, it can't run an independent monetary policy. Governments are thus forced to make a choice: should they prioritize macroeconomic management – the ability to respond to inflation or recession – or stable international trade?

RELATED THEORY
See also
MONETARISM
page 48

3-SECOND BIOGRAPHIES
ROBERT MUNDELL
1932–

JOHN MARCUS FLEMING
1911–1976

30-SECOND TEXT
Katie Huston

'If you look at the international monetary literature when Mundell was in his glory days, you get the impression that he was 15 or 20 years ahead of his contemporaries … He was thinking in terms of a world where money moved freely and massively to wherever it could earn the highest return.'
PAUL KRUGMAN

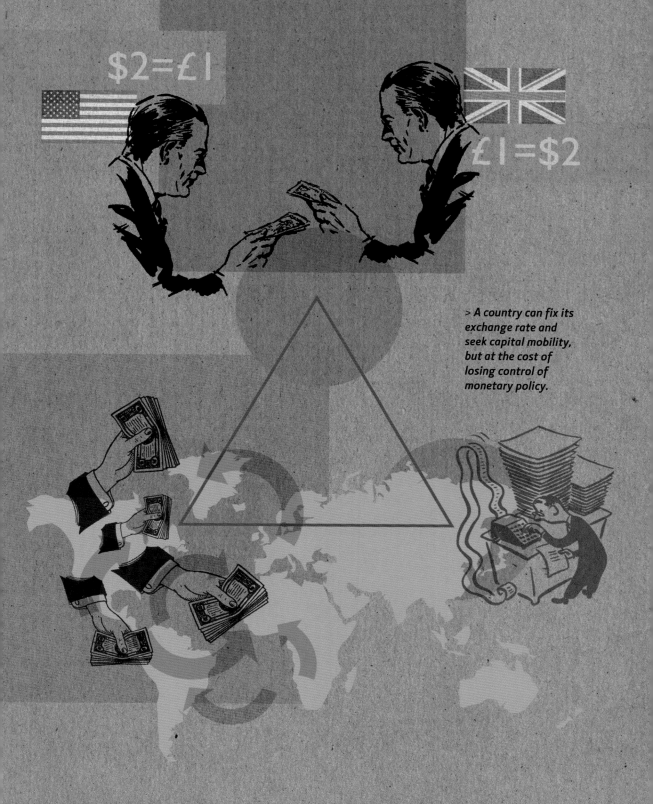

$2=£1

£1=$2

> A country can fix its exchange rate and seek capital mobility, but at the cost of losing control of monetary policy.

PURCHASING POWER PARITY

the 30-second theory

3-SECOND CRASH
Get rid of borders and your burger will cost the same everywhere. If it doesn't, it's because governments play games with exchange rates.

3-MINUTE BOOM
One problem with the theory is that it assumes an ideal borderless world that doesn't exist. The positive side of this is that it gives you a benchmark to compare the value of different currencies. But even this is difficult. How do you compare two economies when what people consume in each country varies so much? The Big Mac Index has been criticized because the demand for McDonald's is not the same in advanced and in developing countries.

What would your dollar be worth in pounds or yen in a world with no borders – or as economists say, where markets are not artificially distorted and can function freely across the globe? In such a world everything would cost the same, no matter where you lived – New York, London or Tokyo. And this would be reflected in the exchange rates of the different currencies. If the same car costs US$15000 in New York and £9000 in London, one US dollar would buy 0.60 pounds. But economics doesn't work like this. Most of the time exchange rates differ from purchasing power parity. In those cases, economists say that one of the currencies is 'undervalued' and the other 'overvalued'. So following the example above, if the exchange rate is one US dollar for 0.5 pounds, then the dollar is undervalued and the pound overvalued. *The Economist* magazine has come up with a yardstick for comparing currencies. This is the famous Big Mac Index, which compares the price in dollars of a Big Mac around the world. In 2009, the most expensive burger was in Norway (US$5.79) while the cheapest was in Malaysia (US$1.70), suggesting these were the most overvalued and undervalued currencies. In the United States, a Big Mac was US$3.54.

RELATED THEORIES
See also
THE IMPOSSIBLE TRINITY
page 98
OPTIMAL CURRENCY AREA
page 96

3-SECOND BIOGRAPHY
KARL GUSTAV CASSEL
1866–1945

30-SECOND TEXT
Christakis Georgiou

'A world currency!'
KARL GUSTAV CASSEL'S
DYING WORDS

> In a truly free global economy, once the exchange rate is taken into account, everything would cost the same.

CHOICE ◐

CHOICE
GLOSSARY

altruism The desire to do good for others without the expectation of personal gain. The concept confounds the widely-held belief that humans are all self-interested individuals focused on maximizing their own rewards, and is difficult to reconcile with most classical economic theory.

behavioural economics An approach to economics that incorporates social and emotional factors in the decision-making process. Whereas previous models had deliberately steered away from psychology to establish economics as a pure science, behavioural economics sought to show that decision making is influenced by such things as framing (see below), intuition and peer pressure. The important conclusion is that decision making is not necessarily an entirely rational process, as is generally assumed.

cost/benefit analysis The decision-making process by which someone decides whether the benefit of something is worth the cost of acquiring/undertaking it.

framing The way in which people perceive the world, and how this view influences their decision making, economic or otherwise. A person's framing can be determined by their upbringing, social environment and education, as well as personal makeup. It can be manipulated by politicians, advertisers and others to influence outcomes.

irrational exuberance A phrase used by former Federal Reserve chairman Alan Greenspan to describe the 1990s stock market boom. The implication was that the market was overvalued and might come down with a bump – a prediction that came true a few years later. The phrase was originated by Robert Shiller and used as the title of his book published in 2000.

lobbyist A person employed to persuade government to adopt policies that will benefit the special interest of a particular group or company. The term is thought to come from the tradition of approaching Members of Parliament while they are gathered in the halls (or 'lobbies') of the Houses of Parliament before and after a debate.

monopoly The dominance of a market by one firm to the exclusion of all others.

risk aversion The dislike of taking risk. A risk-averse person would rather invest their money in a safe option with a lower rate of return (for example, a savings account or government bonds) rather than risk it on the vagaries of the stock market. A less risk-averse person would be more willing to invest in stocks, which offer the potential for higher returns but at greater risk of losses.

subprime Literally, below ('sub') the best ('prime'). The term is applied to loans that carry a higher-than-normal risk of default. There are several reasons why loans might be categorized as 'subprime'. The borrowers might have a low credit rating and/or a history of nonpayment. The loan itself might represent a higher proportion of the asset than is usually recommended (for example, 110 per cent mortgages). The borrower may not have all the documentation usually required (for example, income self-certification).

utility The measure of usefulness a person gains from pursuing a certain action. In economics, this mainly refers to the consumption of goods and services. Classical economics assumes that the individual is uniquely motivated to maximize utility, although subsequent theories have tried to create a more rounded model.

RATIONAL CHOICE

the 30-second theory

People want to be as happy as possible, given the constraints they face. When it comes to making decisions, whether buying a car or planning a holiday, they use all available information and weigh costs and benefits to make a rational choice that will help them attain happiness, known as 'maximizing utility'. In a perfect world, people would have all the information there is about each choice and its outcome, and have the ability and time to weigh each decision against the others – but this is rarely the case. Gary Becker, a key contributor to the theory of rational choice, theorized that rationality isn't the same for everyone, but rather it's based on individual preferences and views, and constrained by time, income, cognitive ability, and access to information. This helps economists analyze decision making under uncertainty; they can model 'rational' behaviour to predict people's future actions, which helps predict larger economic trends. Rational choice is also widely used in politics and sociology. In politics, rational choice has reshaped the study of interest groups, elections and bureaucracy, and provides a way of understanding actions between nations; in sociology (or more specifically criminology), the theory is used to understand why people commit crimes, in order to try to prevent them in the future.

3-SECOND CRASH
People make choices for a reason. Whether choosing a car, a university, or a spouse, they look at all the facts and make a rational judgment.

3-MINUTE BOOM
Becker argued that people use cost/benefit analysis for all choices, including altruism, crime, discrimination, family and household matters, and punishment. Yet committing a murder or becoming an alcoholic doesn't exactly seem rational, and other theories compete with rational choice to explain it. For example, psychological theories argue that people aren't always rational, but use rules of thumb and instinct to make choices. Other theories point out myopia (short-sightedness) and inertia (the tendency not to act).

RELATED THEORIES
See also
CLASSICAL
page 12
RATIONAL EXPECTATIONS
page 56
GAME THEORY
page 108
PUBLIC CHOICE
page 112
EXPECTED UTILITY THEORY
page 114

3-SECOND BIOGRAPHIES
JEREMY BENTHAM
1748–1832

GARY BECKER
1930–

30-SECOND TEXT
Katie Huston

'Individuals maximize welfare as they conceive it, whether they be selfish, altruistic, loyal, spiteful, or masochistic.'

GARY BECKER

> *All the decisions we make in life, whether buying a car or deciding who to marry, are based on weighing up the pros and cons of each option using all the available information.*

GAME THEORY

the 30-second theory

Strategic decisions are made
every day by individuals, firms and governments.
Like any game of strategy, decisions are usually
made with little or no prior knowledge of the
decisions of other players. So, without this
knowledge, how can you choose which
strategies to follow? Game theory has been
used in economics to model decision making
in such a strategic environment. The aim is to
understand strategic interactions where
outcomes for one 'player' depend upon the
choices of others. Most commonly, the theory
assumes that such choices will occur
simultaneously. Each player in the 'game'
will make his or her decision based upon the
expectation of how the others will behave.
Should Microsoft announce the release of its
latest product if it expects that Apple is about
to release something similar? Furthermore,
recent attention has been drawn to cases where
timing is sequential and based upon repeated
games. Repeated interaction means that
companies will not simply base their decisions
upon immediate payoffs, but upon the expected
responses of other players. When, for example,
should Coke decide to lower their prices, given
that Pepsi can respond and spark a price war
in which either both could lose or one could
end up with an increased market share?

3-SECOND CRASH
What do business, love
and war have in common?
They are all games of
strategy.

3-MINUTE BOOM
Game theory advocates
most commonly emphasize
its predictive qualities.
By providing a scientific
means for modelling
human behaviour, it is
claimed that the theory
is a vital tool for
understanding the
complexities of economic
decision making. Yet can
the mathematical model of
strategic interactions really
capture the complex array
of influences acting upon
economic decisions? For
example, the influence of
factors outside the 'game'
may impact profoundly
upon decisions.

RELATED THEORIES
See also
RATIONAL CHOICE
page 106
PUBLIC CHOICE
page 112

3-SECOND BIOGRAPHIES
ANATOL RAPOPORT
1911–2007

JOHN NASH
1928–

30-SECOND TEXT
Adam Fishwick

'*The general who wins
a battle makes many
calculations in his
temple 'ere the battle
is fought. The general
who loses a battle
makes but few
calculations
beforehand. Thus
do many calculations
lead to victory, and few
calculations to defeat:
how much more no
calculation at all!*'
SUN TZU

> *Strategic decisions should be made on the presumed actions and reactions of other players in the game. It's your move.*

1930
Born, Pottsville, Pennsylvania

1951
BA at Princeton University

1954
Marries Doria Slote

1955
PhD at University of Chicago

1957
Publishes *The Economics of Discrimination*

1958
Professor of Economics at University of Columbia

1970
Professor of Economics at University of Chicago

1980
Marries Guity Nashat

1981
Publishes *A Treatise on the Family*

1983
Professor of Sociology at University of Chicago

1985–2004
Monthly column in *Business Week*

1992
Awarded Nobel Prize for Economics

2007
Awarded Presidential Medal of Freedom by George Bush Jr

GARY BECKER

Are children a better investment than a retirement fund? Do people deliberately discriminate against others by hiking up the price of transactions when selling to a different ethnic group? Do criminals rationally weigh up the financial gains of committing a crime against the punishment they might receive if caught? Are wealthy couples more likely to stay together than poor couples because the cost of divorce is so much greater? Such questions are hardly the staple of conventional economic theory, yet they are some of the issues addressed by Gary Becker in a lifetime of fusing the often antagonistic disciplines of economics and sociology.

Born in Pottsville, Pennsylvania, in 1930, his interest in economics started when he had to read his father the business news due to his father's failing eyesight. His practical application of often abstract economic theories was encouraged by the economist Milton Friedman, who lectured him at Chicago University in the 1950s. His first paper putting these theories into practice was initially rejected by the *Journal of Political Economy*, however, and it would be years before his approach was, albeit grudgingly, accepted into the mainstream. His first book, *The Economics of Discrimination* – analyzing the impact of prejudice on the employment of racial minorities – was published in 1957 to mixed reviews, although it is now widely regarded as a landmark publication. One of his most controversial theories was the 'rotten kid theorem' published in his *A Treatise on the Family*, which posits that even a 'rotten kid' will behave well towards his or her sibling in order to secure a greater share of the parents' benevolence. Economics, he suggested, operates even within family relationships.

By the 1990s, the rest of the world had caught up with Becker and he was awarded the Nobel Prize for Economics. His 'Dr Seuss' approach has since been widely adopted in a series of popular books on economics, such as *Freakonomics*, *The Economic Naturalist*, and *The Undercover Economist*.

PUBLIC CHOICE
the 30-second theory

Public choice theorists apply the
logic of rational choice theory to the political
sphere. They think political actors and economic
actors behave in the same way – they both seek
to maximize their personal interest. Political
theorists often treat the state as a complete
entity, whereas public choice theorists consider
all action in the political sphere to be the result
of the behaviour of self-interested individuals.
For public choice theorists, policies are a direct
result of the decisions made by bureaucrats and
politicians seeking to be re-elected or to get
a better salary, for example. If politics follows
the same rules that apply to economic markets,
you would expect it to be similarly efficient.
However, competition, which ensures efficiency
in the economic market, is less present in the
political arena. For example, the politicians and
bureaucrats in charge of agricultural affairs have
a monopoly on agricultural policy decisions –
they have complete control over how their
budget is spent. As a result, rather than policy
decisions being made in the general interest,
they tend to reflect the particular interests of
political actors. Hence, public choice theorists
often conclude that less intervention in the
economy is better. Besides looking at
bureaucracy, public choice scholars also
study the paradoxes of voting systems
and the role of political parties and lobbies.

3-SECOND CRASH
Politicians are people
too. They may talk
about the public good,
but they have their
own personal agendas.

3-MINUTE BOOM
Public choice is often
criticized for being too
narrow. However, public
choice theorists argue
that even altruistic or
humanitarian motives can
be explained as egoistic.
The pursuit of public
interest is thus possible,
but only if it matches
private interests! Public
choice theorists also
believe they analyze
political action with
neutral scientific tools,
but such theorists are
often associated with
their own political
agenda, which favours
small government.

RELATED THEORIES
See also
RATIONAL CHOICE
page 106
GAME THEORY
page 108
RENT SEEKING
page 154

3-SECOND BIOGRAPHIES
JAMES BUCHANAN
1919–

GORDON TULLOCK
1922–

GEORGE STIGLER
1911–1991

30-SECOND TEXT
Aurélie Maréchal

' … if you want to
improve politics,
improve the rules,
improve the structure.
Don't expect
politicians to behave
differently. They
behave according
to their interests.'
JAMES BUCHANAN

> Politicians are often more concerned about getting re-elected than they are about the public good. Voters are more concerned about their wallets.

EXPECTED UTILITY THEORY
the 30-second theory

How would you choose in which stock to invest your money, given that you can't be certain of what's going to happen in the future? Would you choose the biotech start-up that might deliver a breakthrough drug ten years from now but will be worthless otherwise? Or would you choose the staid electric utility that has provided moderate returns for decades? As well as considering the likelihood of the biotech company doing well, you also should consider how scared you are of losing your money if things don't work out (economists call this risk aversion). If losing money would make you very unhappy (reduce your utility in economics-speak), then you are better off investing in the electric utility. And if you don't care about gains on the stock market, you might as well skip both investments and buy a season ticket for your football team or a new car. According to economists von Neumann and Morgenstern, this can be summed up in a mathematical formula that reflects the way people make decisions under uncertainty. Their theory improves on previous 'expected value' theories. 'Expected value' theories only took into account the first two criteria – possible return and probability of that happening. But that is not enough – you also need to account for how happy gains make people and how unhappy losses make them.

RELATED THEORIES
See also
RATIONAL CHOICE
page 106
GAME THEORY
page 108
PROSPECT THEORY
page 116

3-SECOND BIOGRAPHIES
JOHN VON NEUMANN
1903–1957
OSKAR MORGENSTERN
1902–1977

30-SECOND TEXT
Christakis Georgiou

3-SECOND CRASH
How do people make decisions in the face of uncertainty? By weighing the probabilities of possible outcomes and how happy each of those outcomes would make them.

3-MINUTE BOOM
The theory sounds simple and great. But how realistic is it to assume that people invest solely based on a rational assessment of probabilities and potential outcomes. After all, Alan Greenspan, head of the Federal Reserve Board from 1988 to 2006, called the 1990s a period of 'irrational exuberance' because the way investors gambled on financial markets seemed to be cut off from reality and the prospect of potential gains. The subprime bubble was another instance of this.

'Nothing is more difficult, and therefore more precious, than being able to decide.'
NAPOLEON BONAPARTE

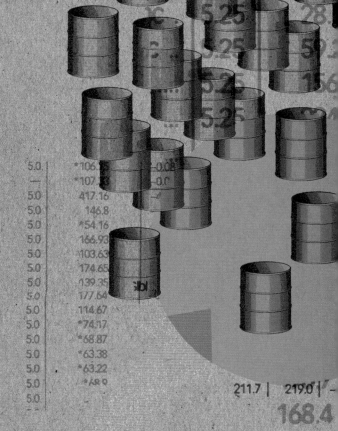

> *Just think how happy you'll be when your investment comes off – or how unhappy you'll feel if it doesn't. It affects how we make our decisions.*

5.0	*106.25	-0.08
—	*107.33	-0.0
5.0	417.16	
5.0	146.8	
5.0	*54.16	
5.0	166.93	
5.0	103.63	
5.0	174.65	
5.0	139.35	
5.0	177.64	
5.0	114.67	
5.0	*74.17	
5.0	*68.87	
5.0	*63.38	
5.0	*63.22	
5.0	*68.9	
5.0		

211.7 | 219.0 |

168.4

......	3.5	108.9
......	3.5	*21.92
......	—	*38.47
......	—	*29.65
ts		
...	3.5	282.2
.	3.5	177.4
		49.02

80.7

28.54

59.24

156.6

924.8

1553.0

78.23

166.7

43.38

541.6

PROSPECT THEORY

the 30-second theory

Most of modern mainstream economic thinking is based on models operating according to rational choice assumptions – as in the case of expected utility theory examined earlier. But in the early 1980s Daniel Kahneman and Amos Tversky developed another theory – the prospect theory. This explained that the way people frame decisions can have a huge effect on how they make choices. In other words, choices don't depend solely on potential outcomes and probabilities, as rational choice assumes, but also on how the choices are presented. Cancer patients, for example, may prefer a treatment that offers a nine in ten chance of living to one that offers a one in ten chance of dying, even though, objectively, they are identical. Framing is a subjective process by which people attribute value to one choice or the other. The key difference with expected utility is that not everyone has the same way of framing choices. So, even if two people are equally afraid of making the wrong choice, they might choose different things because they frame each choice differently. Prospect theory brings together economics and psychology – both Kahneman and Tversky were academic specialists in psychology – and it is part of a school of economic thought called 'behaviourial economics'.

RELATED THEORIES
See also
EXPECTED UTILITY THEORY
page 114
RATIONAL CHOICE
page 106

3-SECOND BIOGRAPHIES
DANIEL KAHNEMAN
1934–

AMOS TVERSKY
1937–1996

30-SECOND TEXT
Christakis Georgiou

3-SECOND CRASH
How do people make decisions in the face of uncertainty? By comparing possible outcomes to where they stand today (or, at least, where they think they stand).

3-MINUTE BOOM
This theory seems to be a useful extension to the assumptions of expected utility theory. But once you've accepted framing plays a role in decision making, you need to explain what determines framing – that is the processes that make people value one thing more than another. That seems to have more to do with sociology or even psychology than economics. That's not a problem, although it suggests that answers to real world problems come from interdisciplinary approaches.

'People assign much higher probability to the truth of their opinions than is warranted. It's one of the reasons people trade so much in the market, generally with bad results.'
DANIEL KAHNEMAN

> It's often our perception of how the choices are presented rather than the choices themselves that make us arrive at our decisions.

TAX & SPEND POLICIES

aggregate demand The total demand for goods and services within an economy at a certain time. This can be influenced by government either through monetary policy (that is controlling the amount of money in the economy through interest rates) and/or fiscal policy (that is increasing/decreasing the amount of government expenditure).

bond A form of security for a debt. Typically, the issuer sells bonds to raise finance for investment. In return, they are obliged to pay interest to the holder of the bonds until the bonds 'mature', at which point the issuers repays the original sum, and the debt is cleared. Bonds are usually issued by governments, banks and corporations with typical terms of five to thirty years.

capital gains The difference between the purchase price and the selling price (in other words the profit) of capital assets, such as property, stocks and bonds, and artworks. Capital gains are usually taxed at a different rate to normal income tax and in some cases may be exempt from tax.

deadweight loss The loss in efficiency created by the artificial manipulation of a market, for example, through a monopoly or subsidy. Thus, if a company has a monopoly of a product and overcharges for it, the 'deadweight loss' is the loss in business created by turning away customers who would have bought the product if it were fairly priced. Conversely, if a product is subsidized to below its market value, the 'deadweight loss' is the expenditure of customers who buy the product because it is cheap but who wouldn't buy it at its normal market value.

deficit The government spending more than it collects in tax revenues.

elasticity This is a measure of the desirability of a product or service and, therefore, the flexibility of its price. A highly elastic product or service is one that customers can do without or which is widely available, therefore, a small change in the price will influence whether they buy it or not. An inelastic product or service is one that customers consider essential and/or is not widely available, and that they will buy even if the price is raised considerably.

fiscal policy The use of public spending and taxation to influence a country's economic performance. This may typically involve raising taxation and/or selling government bonds to pay for public works and services.

Harberger triangle A diagram that measures the effect of 'deadweight loss' (see above) on a market. Named after the economist Arnold Harberger.

liquidity The ability of an asset to be bought and sold without any great loss in value.

recession A period during which a country's economy contracts. Typical symptoms of a recession are: a reduction in consumer spending, reduced capital investment, an increase in bankruptcies, and a rise in unemployment. A common measurement for recession is a fall in gross domestic product (GDP) for at least two quarters in a row. Typical government remedies are stimulus packages, including increasing the supply of money and/or increasing government expenditure.

stimulus Measures used to reinvigorate a flagging economy. This typically takes the form of increasing the supply of money, lowering tax, and/or increased government expenditure.

supply-side The part of the economy that 'supplies' products and services, in other words, corporations and their employees. Supply-side theories focus on making the economy conducive to business and minimizing government regulation.

TAX INCIDENCE

the 30-second theory

Suppose a government wants to tax petrol but is worried about angering voters. The government might decide to tax the petrol companies rather than consumers. It seems ingenious – taxing big, bad oil companies rather than the voting public – but there's one catch: producers don't want to bear the tax either, and so they increase their prices. Consumers still end up paying at least some of the tax, even though they aren't the ones writing a cheque to the government. But producers can't necessarily pass on the entire tax. If they try, they might not be able to get rid of all of the products they have for sale. So they have to compromise and charge a price that only partly compensates for the tax. You get a situation where the burden of taxation is borne partly by the producer and partly by the consumer. But what determines who bears how much of the burden? Economists say this depends on the 'elasticity' of the supply and demand for a certain product. 'Elasticity' is a measure of how much you stay with a product when its price rises. If consumers perceive a product to be essential or 'inelastic', they will be prepared to pay more of the tax than producers. But if consumers don't really care about a product it's said to be elastic – and then it's up to the producer to bear the burden.

3-SECOND CRASH
A tax on someone else may really be a tax on you – you are paying more in taxes than you think.

3-MINUTE BOOM
Goods such as cigarettes, alcohol, and petrol have very inelastic demand. Few people can get by without their daily smoke, beer, or fuel for their car to get to work in the morning. It's not very easy either for producers to quickly adjust the supply of these things. So governments play it smart by heavily taxing the consumption of these products.

RELATED THEORY
See also
EXCESS BURDEN
page 124

3-SECOND BIOGRAPHY
RICHARD MUSGRAVE
1910–2007

30-SECOND TEXT
Christakis Georgiou

'There is no such thing as a good tax.'
WINSTON CHURCHILL

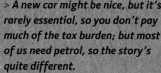

> A new car might be nice, but it's rarely essential, so you don't pay much of the tax burden; but most of us need petrol, so the story's quite different.

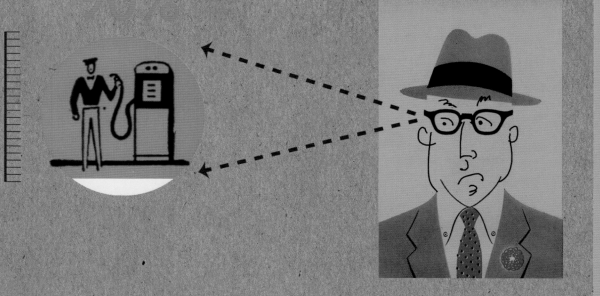

EXCESS BURDEN

the 30-second theory

3-SECOND CRASH
Taxes cost more than just the money the government gets out of us. It's also all those things we would have consumed but don't because of the tax.

3-MINUTE BOOM
One important assumption of the theory is that markets are usually perfect. But if one follows the neo-Keynesians (*see page 20*) and accepts their starting point, which is that in the real world, markets are rarely perfect, then taxes become a way of correcting imperfections. Some economists argue that taxes are useful because they can redistribute income from the rich to the poor. They say a fairer distribution of income is more conducive to growth.

Excess burden due to taxation is an example of what economists call deadweight loss. This occurs when the price of a product does not reflect the equilibrium between supply and demand. Say coffee is sold at a price above equilibrium because the seller monopolizes the market. Starbucks or Costa Coffee will make surplus profits. But people will buy fewer cups of coffee because it is more pricey. The surplus profit made by Starbucks or Costa Coffee will be lower than the value of the cups of coffee that we didn't indulge in. This difference is the deadweight loss. It's certainly great for Starbucks or Costa Coffee, but on the whole bad for the economy. Excess burden happens when governments impose taxes on goods or services. This tax will be passed on to the consumer by an increase in the price of the product sold. The government will get the extra bit of money this time around. But because of the higher price due to the tax, people will buy less of the product than they would have otherwise done. The same as above applies, with the government benefitting instead of the monopoly. The trouble is that according to the theory, if tax rates double, the excess burden will probably quadruple.

RELATED THEORIES
See also
TAX INCIDENCE
page 122
MARGINALISM
page 138

3-SECOND BIOGRAPHY
ARNOLD HARBERGER
1924–

30-SECOND TEXT
Christakis Georgiou

'On the other hand, there is almost no economic event where supply and demand does not enter. So if you really know how to handle supply and demand, put it into different contexts at different times, you're way ahead of the game.'

ARNOLD HARBERGER

> Too much tax and people will stop being able to buy things – and that's a deadweight loss for the economy as a whole.

1842
Born, Bermondsey, London

1865
Mathematical Tripos, St John's College, Cambridge

1877
Marries Mary Paley

1877
Professor of Political Economy, University College, Bristol

1879
Publishes *The Economics of Industry*

1883
Professor of Political Economy, Oxford

1884
Professor of Political Economy, Cambridge

1890
Publishes *Principles of Economics*

1908
Retires

1919
Publishes *Industry and Trade*

1923
Publishes *Money, Credit, and Commerce*

1924
Dies, Cambridge

ALFRED MARSHALL

A fussy, obsessive man, fixated on detail and prone to turning his best friends into enemies because of his lack of flexibility – these are not the characteristics most likely to sweep someone to the top of their profession. Yet Alfred Marshall was all these things. The most respected economist of his generation, he wrote many of the theorems that form the foundations of the subject to this day. Yet his continual procrastination and agonizing over details severely limited his output and, arguably, meant he only achieved a fraction of his potential. By the end of his tenure, John Maynard Keynes was just one of his one-time friends who became disillusioned and alienated by him.

Born in 1842 in Bermondsey, London, Marshall had originally intended to become a clergyman, but success at Cambridge University set him on an academic trajectory. Economics was still in its infancy then, and Marshall determined to give it a more scientific basis and establish it as an independent discipline. He was also keen to make the subject accessible to the layman and, therefore, buried much of the technical detail of his texts in footnotes and appendices. His *Economics of Industry*, cowritten with his wife and former student Mary Paley, brought immediate recognition when it was published in 1879. It was followed by *Principles of Economics*, published in 1890 after nearly ten years' of hard work, which established the principles of supply and demand, marginal utility, and the costs of production – all of which have become standard models in economic theory. Marshall spent twenty years working on his next volume, continually rewriting it as the world changed around him, but was unable to complete it due to deteriorating health. Instead, he published lesser works, such as *Industry and Trade* and *Money, Credit, and Commerce*, which failed to recreate his earlier success. After years of badgering, however, he did succeed in 1903 in creating a separate department for Economics at Cambridge University. Thanks in great part to his efforts, economics was now a subject worthy of obsession.

SUPPLY-SIDE ECONOMICS

the 30-second theory

Not everyone agrees that strong growth depends on strong aggregate demand. In the latter part of the 1970s, economists such as Robert Mundell and Arthur Laffer, and journalist and conservative Jude Wanniski reasoned that the solution was to return to the classical economists' focus on the supply side. They argued that this meant tax cuts for everyone, especially high-income earners and on capital gains. Because of the cuts, investors would get to keep a higher proportion of the returns on their investments and workers' take-home wage would increase. The former would then have an incentive to invest more and the latter to work more. This would increase productivity, put more goods and services on the market, and drive prices down. In turn, this would lead to higher growth. Some supply-siders even argued this would mean higher tax revenues for the government. What about inflation? Because of higher levels of economic activity, all the extra money in the economy would be put to productive use and inflation would disappear. Supply-side economics is strongly associated with the first presidency of Ronald Reagan. It is also very popular with many members of the US Republican Party, who traditionally oppose high federal taxes and state intervention.

3-SECOND CRASH
Greater growth depends on greater incentives for those who invest and for those who work. Governments should tax everyone less.

3-MINUTE BOOM
The most extreme supply-side claims – that tax cuts would lead to higher tax revenues – never panned out. Indeed, deficits ballooned during the Reagan years and have been a challenge ever since (except for a brief period in the late 1990s). Also, as many critics have noted, the usual supply-side recommendations of lower taxes tend to favour the wealthy and high-income earners. How should the potential growth benefits of supply-side policies be balanced against such distributional concerns?

RELATED THEORY
See also
KEYNESIAN ECONOMICS
(NORMATIVE)
page 46

3-SECOND BIOGRAPHIES
ROBERT MUNDELL
1932–

ARTHUR LAFFER
1940–

JUDE WANNISKI
1936–2005

30-SECOND TEXT
Christakis Georgiou

'The poor have become fat and happy, the rich impoverished. This is why we are in the fix we are in. Everyone wants to be poor, because it has so many more advantages!'

JUDE WANNISKI

> Cut people free from the
burden of high taxation
and they'll be incentivized
to work harder.

CROWDING OUT

the 30-second theory

3-SECOND CRASH
When governments spend money, it has to come from somewhere – and it often comes out of the private sector's pockets.

3-MINUTE BOOM
Stimulus advocates say that in a recession, savings rates are higher and capital is not being fully utilized, so crowding out won't be a problem. However, critics argue that although government injections of cash can help in the short term, in the long run they may lead to economic slowdown, rather than recovery. It also depends on how government spends the money; investment in infrastructure, education, and health are more likely to have positive long-term, supply-side effects.

When governments spend money, where does that money come from? A lot of it comes from taxes, but when they can't quite foot the bill, governments borrow from the money market by issuing bonds. With government now competing with firms and individuals to borrow, the increased demand for loans raises interest rates. What's more, when people's savings are in government bonds, less wealth is available to finance private investment. The bottom line? When government pulls out its wallet, it can 'crowd out' private investment, borrowing and savings. Loans get more expensive, and there aren't as many to go around, so corporations and people can't afford to borrow money. The solution? Reduce deficits. Most economists agree that crowding out is a problem when economies are performing well. In times of economic downturn, however, the debate gets more heated. Many economists follow Keynes, who believed that spending in a downturn has a 'multiplier effect', when an injection of cash boosts consumption, which leads to more investment and job creation, which leads to more consumption. Thus spending creates repeated rounds of spending, a virtuous circle of growth, and national income increases over and beyond the amount of money government forked out up front – the classic argument in favour of a stimulus.

RELATED THEORIES
See also
CLASSICAL
page 12
NEOCLASSICAL SYNTHESIS
page 20
KEYNESIAN ECONOMICS
(NORMATIVE)
page 46
MONETARISM
page 48

3-SECOND BIOGRAPHY
ROBERT RUBIN
1938 –

30-SECOND TEXT
Katie Huston

'Government spending financed by taxes or borrowing from saving of the general public may reduce other spending to such an extent that there will be little, if any, net increase in total spending.'

**ROGER W. SPENCER
AND WILLIAM P. YOHE**

> If governments try to spend their way out of a recession, investment cash can dry up.

MARKETS

MARKETS
GLOSSARY

caveat emptor Latin for 'let the buyer beware'. A principle whereby the seller is not responsible for any failures in a property or product once a sale has been completed. It is, therefore, up to the buyer to check for defects before making the purchase. The only exception is if defects are actively concealed – although even then it is up to the buyer to prove that this is the case.

caveat venditor Latin for 'let the seller beware', meaning that the seller accepts responsibility for ensuring a property or product is fit for purpose and consistent with the description in a contract, even after the sale is completed. Increasingly, modern consumer protection laws tend to apply this principle.

due diligence Originally a term used by stock brokers accused of not disclosing sufficient information about stocks and shares. The idea is that, as long as someone has carried out adequate investigations and disclosed all the relevant information to the client, they cannot be held responsible for not disclosing information that they themselves did not know about. The term is now commonly used in nonfinancial situations.

dynamic economy A system in a constant state of innovation and development. Capitalism is arguably the most dynamic economic system because of its focus on the market mechanism, which demands that producers and manufacturers respond swiftly to changes in economic conditions.

general equilibrium theory The idea that the price of all goods and services within an economy are interrelated and balanced. This means that a change in the price of one item can have consequences on the prices of millions of others. A typical example is the price of bread, which affects the baker's wages, which influences his choice of vehicle. If the public's taste for bread changes, this starts a chain reaction that is almost impossible to predict. The market mechanism, however, ensures that balance is eventually restored.

market mechanism A theoretical system whereby supply, demand and price achieve perfect equilibrium. The principle is that as demand for a product increases, the price will increase, too, until supply exceeds demand. At this point, the price will decrease until supply and demand balance out again. This is the principle on which all market-led systems are based.

Marxism A political theory devised by Karl Marx and Friedrich Engels. The main precept is that all history can be defined in terms of the class struggle between the working class and the bourgeoisie. Marx believed that capitalists make their profit through exploiting the working class, and that revolution by workers would be the inevitable result of this unequal relationship.

privatization Mainly, the sale of publicly owned assets (that is enterprises and property owned by the state) into private hands. This might include assets, such as railways, utility companies and even hospitals. Increasingly, the term refers to the outsourcing of government services to private companies, including everything from school meals to revenue collection and prison services.

protectionism The practice of protecting domestic trade against foreign competition by imposing quotas and tariffs on incoming goods. This is usually done to ensure a positive balance of payments, where imports of foreign goods threaten to outweigh exports of locally-produced goods. It may also be done to protect a nascent industry, such as car manufacturing in Japan in the 1930s and 1940s.

quotas Quotas are used to divide scarce resources among interested parties, or to limit the output of undesirable emissions. They are widely used in conjunction with cap-and-trade schemes, whereby countries or companies are allowed to 'trade' quotas among themselves.

self-regulation The principle whereby agents are allowed to set standards for themselves, instead of being dictated to by central government. The theory goes that the market mechanism will automatically encourage good practice and destroy bad practice.

sustainable Managing resources within the capacity of the planet to replenish them.

THE INVISIBLE HAND

the 30-second theory

3-SECOND CRASH
To create more wealth, just help yourself.

3-MINUTE BOOM
Seems simple enough – but does it work? Not always. Even Adam Smith recognized that self-interest for wealth creation had its limits, and believed government had to step in when it came to protecting private property and providing public goods, such as roads. Take environmental goods as an example: Hardin's 'tragedy of the commons' theory shows that when multiple actors using a shared resource pursue individual gain, the resource will be depleted unless strong property rights are in place.

A butcher doesn't sell meat because he's altruistic; he slices and dices to turn a profit. But to sell the meat, he needs to pay attention to what his customers want. Thus to pursue his own wealth, the butcher serves the needs of society – and in a market economy, according to Adam Smith, most people behave the same way. That is, when people can choose freely what to produce and what to buy, the 'invisible hand' of competition guides the exchange of goods and services so that personal greed leads to collective gain. For example, when entrepreneurs want to attract more business, they offer lower prices. It's a win-win game and a dynamic, self-regulating process that occurs and adjusts automatically. Smith used this theory to argue against government regulation and protectionism in a market economy – although for the invisible hand to work properly, society must have strong property rights, established legal and moral codes, and the exchange of information. Smith is often considered the 'father of economics', and for good reason. His theory of the invisible hand, coined in his 1776 book *The Wealth of Nations*, guided the era of classical economics for more than 150 years and still shapes the economic debate today.

RELATED THEORIES
see also
CLASSICAL
page 12
FREE MARKET CAPITALISM
page 28
THE TRAGEDY OF
THE COMMONS
page 142
PROPERTY RIGHTS
page 144

3-SECOND BIOGRAPHIES
ADAM SMITH
1723-1790
DAVID RICARDO
1772-1823

30-SECOND TEXT
Katie Huston

'It is not from the benevolence of the butcher, the brewer, or the baker that we expect our dinner, but from their regard to their own self-interest.'

ADAM SMITH

> The butcher doesn't sell meat because you need to put food on your table; he sells meat because he needs to put food on his table.

MARGINALISM

the 30-second theory

One of the oldest debates in economics is the value controversy. Early political economists, such as Adam Smith, held that it is the average amount of labour time necessary to make a product that determines its value. Against this 'labour theory of value', late nineteenth-century economists, such as William Stanley Jevons and Alfred Marshall, argued that it is the marginal utility of a product that determines its value. This 'exchange theory of value' is based on the idea that people will derive less enjoyment from the consumption of every extra unit of a product that they consume. You might like apples, but you won't keep eating them until they run out. At some point you'll be fed up with them and start eating something else instead. But how does this relate to the price of things? Take, for example, the paradox of water and diamonds. Water is essential to people for their survival, whereas diamonds aren't. But water, although essential to life, is far cheaper than diamonds. This is because globally water is abundant in a way that makes little difference whether you have an extra gallon of it or not. Its price is, therefore, low. Diamonds, on the other hand, are rare – and having a diamond or not makes a huge difference in financial terms. Therefore, its price is high.

RELATED THEORY
See also
THE INVISIBLE HAND
page 136

3-SECOND BIOGRAPHIES
WILLIAM STANLEY JEVONS
1835–1882

ALFRED MARSHALL
1842–1924

30-SECOND TEXT
Christakis Georgiou

3-SECOND CRASH
It's not the 'importance' of a product, but the combination of its abundance and desirability that determines its price.

3-MINUTE BOOM
The theory sounds on target. But can it really explain everything that happens? It assumes an equilibrium where supply and demand meet, but in reality this equilibrium is very rarely reached and maintained. Nor does the theory say what happens to demand and supply over time – it doesn't explain change. It is a static theory, whereas capitalism is the most dynamic economic system in human history.

'Again, most of the chief distinctions marked by economic terms are differences not of kind but of degree.'
ALFRED MARSHALL

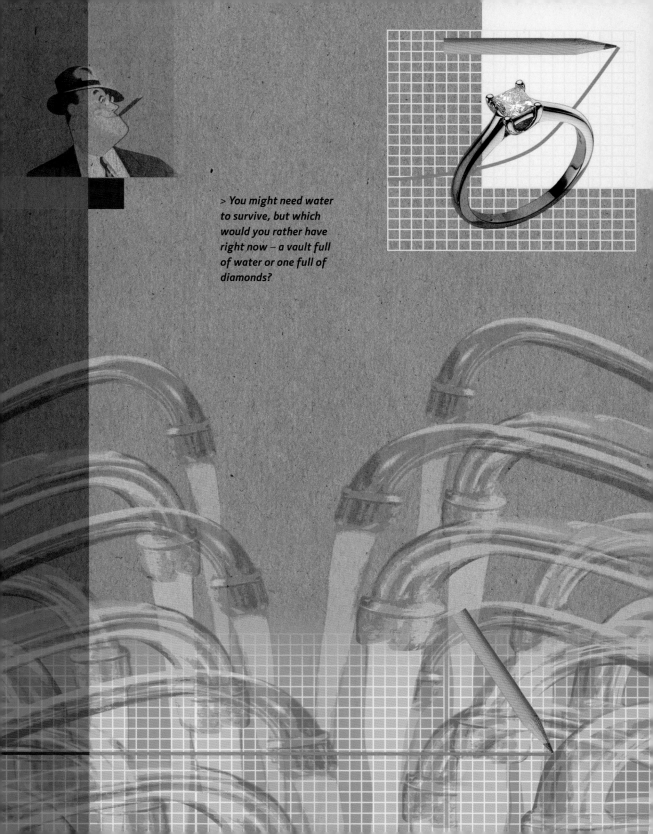

> *You might need water to survive, but which would you rather have right now – a vault full of water or one full of diamonds?*

1723
Born, Kirkcaldy, Fife, Scotland

1737
Studies moral philosophy at University
of Glasgow

1740
Attends Balliol College, Oxford, England

1751
Professor of Logic at University of Glasgow

1752
Professor of Moral Philosophy at University
of Glasgow

1759
Publishes *The Theory of Moral Sentiments*

1763
Tutors Henry Scott, future Duke of Buccleuch

1773
Elected fellow of the Royal Society of London

1776
Publishes *An Inquiry Into the Nature and
Causes of the Wealth of Nations*

1778
Appointed Commissioner of Customs
in Scotland

1787
Appointed Lord Rector of University
of Glasgow

1790
Dies, Edinburgh, Scotland

ADAM SMITH

Everyone loves Adam Smith.

Often described as 'the father of economics', he is quoted by politicians of wildly different camps to validate their policies. To the right-wingers he is the defender of the free market and a stout campaigner against government legislation; to the left-wingers he is the originator of the labour theory of value, which is central to Marxist thinking. Whatever your political persuasion, it seems, quoting Adam Smith gives your cause credibility.

Yet, in company, Smith made an unlikely hero. Born in 1723 in Kirkcaldy, County Fife, Scotland, he was the child of Margaret Douglas and Adam Smith. His father, a lawyer, died six months before Smith was born, and he became very close to his mother. Smith studied moral philosophy at Glasgow University and then Oxford University, before being made Professor of Logic and then Moral Philosophy at Glasgow University. Not a handsome man, he was distinguished by a large nose, bulging eyes, and protruding lower lip. On top of that, he was afflicted with nervous twitches and a speech impediment, and often spoke out loud to himself. As he said of himself: 'I am a beau in nothing but my books.'

Smith's reputation was sealed, however, with the publication of *The Theory of Moral Sentiments* in 1759, in which he argued that people made 'moral' decisions from feelings of sympathy for others. In 1764, he became personal tutor to the future Duke of Buccleuch and travelled around France and Switzerland, where he met influential figures, such as Voltaire, Benjamin Franklin, and François Quesnay. It was while living in Toulouse, which he found boring, that Smith started writing a book 'to pass away the time'. It was to become *An Inquiry Into the Nature and Causes of the Wealth of Nations*, the book that launched the classical strand of economics.

After his tour of Europe, Smith returned to Kirkcaldy, where he lived with his mother until her death in 1784. He died a bachelor six years later.

THE TRAGEDY OF THE COMMONS

the 30-second theory

3-SECOND CRASH
When resources are shared but limited, no one acts to preserve them – which means rational actions can prove irrational in the long run.

3-MINUTE BOOM
Capitalism's critics offer the tragedy of the commons as proof that the invisible hand doesn't always work. But how to regulate it? Hardin believed altruism and common sense wouldn't work, and that private property rights are the best way to manage common resources; governments should limit resource use – such as limiting fishing permits – or common goods, such as water, should be privatized. However, economist Elinor Ostrom challenged this view by showing how many communities do manage resources sustainably over the long term – a contribution that earned her a 2009 Nobel Prize.

Several herders graze their cows on common pasture. From each herder's point of view, it's rational to add more cows to his herd, because his profits will increase. However, every additional cow depletes the pasture's resources. If every farmer acts 'rationally' by adding more cows to his herd, the common land will eventually be overgrazed, grass will stop growing, and all the herders will suffer. In essence, actions that are rational for the individual may be irrational for the group. Yet from each farmer's point of view, buying more cows is rational, because he as an individual reaps all the benefits they bring, while the negative impact is split equally among all the farmers. Garrett Hardin used this example to illustrate 'the tragedy of the commons' in an influential article published in 1968. The term can be applied to the consequences of any situation in which a limited resource is treated as common property and, as a result, may become overused. The tragedy is commonly found in environmental issues, such as overfishing and pollution. This depletion of common resources is an example of an economic externality, or side effect – for example, pollution from a factory can impose cleanup costs on people who live nearby.

RELATED THEORIES
See also
FREE MARKET CAPITALISM
page 28
THE RULE OF LAW
page 80
LIMITS TO GROWTH
page 82
RATIONAL CHOICE
page 106
PROPERTY RIGHTS
page 144
POLLUTER PAYS PRINCIPLE
page 146

3-SECOND BIOGRAPHIES
GARRETT HARDIN
1915–2003

ELINOR OSTROM
1933–

30-SECOND TEXT
Katie Huston

'The inherent logic of the commons remorselessly generates tragedy.'
GARRETT HARDIN

> When individuals are granted free access to the world's resources, the world's resources had better watch out.

PROPERTY RIGHTS

the 30-second theory

3-SECOND CRASH
Missing property rights?
Inefficient markets.

3-MINUTE BOOM
Even if private property is central to the functioning of the capitalist system, not everything can be privately owned. Certain essential public goods and services, such as roads or national defence, need to be provided by the government because private companies would be unable to make a profit from them. Some economists believe certain public services, such as public transport or electricity, can be provided more efficiently through private companies, others argue this is not the case.

Property rights give the owner exclusive authority on a good, a company, a piece of land, or even an intellectual creation. The owner, whether an individual or a government, acquires the exclusive right to use the good, earn income from it, sell it, or transfer it. Well-defined property rights are a fundamental part of the capitalist economic system. In some cases, however, property rights are difficult to define for practical or historical reasons, and can lead markets astray. Too much pollution? That's because there aren't well-defined property rights to the air. Fisheries overharvested? That's because fishermen are competing for the same shared resource. Because commodities, such as air and fish, are not owned by anyone, no one can restrict their usage. Solution? Create property rights. From tradable permits that cover air pollution, to tradable fishing quotas, economists have long advised governments on how to create property rights. The use of the commodities becomes restricted to the person in possession of the permit, so that the overall use of the resource can be capped. As these permits then become tradable, a market is created, which determines a price for the use of the resource.

RELATED THEORIES
See also
THE TRAGEDY OF THE COMMONS
page 142
POLLUTER PAYS PRINCIPLE
page 146

3-SECOND BIOGRAPHIES
RONALD COASE
1910–

ARMEN ALCHIAN
1914–

30-SECOND TEXT
Aurélie Maréchal

'*Private property rights are the rights of humans to use specified goods and to exchange them. Any restraint on private property rights shifts the balance of power from impersonal attributes towards personal attributes and towards behaviour that political authorities approve.*'
ARMEN ALCHIAN

> *Restricting a smash-and-grab free-for-all through the creation of property rights will preserve the use of any given resource.*

POLLUTER PAYS PRINCIPLE

the 30-second theory

RELATED THEORY
See also
PROPERTY RIGHTS
page 144

3-SECOND BIOGRAPHY
ARTHUR CECIL PIGOU
1877–1959

30-SECOND TEXT
Aurélie Maréchal

3-SECOND CRASH
If you are polluting, you should be paying.

3-MINUTE BOOM
The polluter pays principle was first adopted by the OECD in 1972 as one of the first steps towards environmental protection by public authorities. It was recognized by the European Union (1987), and at the major UN Conference on Environment and Development in Rio (1992). Even if the price of pollution is difficult to determine, the polluter pays principle is still central to international environmental law.

A toy factory, as a result of its production process, releases toxins into an adjacent stream. These toxins kill the local fish and sicken anyone who swims in the stream; the factory, however, fails to compensate any of the victims. The factory's private costs of production, therefore, don't reflect the true social costs of its operation. The idea of the polluter pays principle (PPP) is that the toy factory should, in fact, bear the full costs of its actions. This means that the damages caused by the pollution – the lost value to potential fishermen and swimmers – should be included in the cost of production. The PPP puts a price on pollution and attributes the responsibility for it to the polluter. The PPP is based on a fundamental tenet of economic efficiency – that prices should reflect all the costs of production – and sits well with ethical principles of equity and responsibility. Various legal instruments can be used to apply the PPP, and prevent or regulate pollution. These instruments often take the form of taxes (often called Pigouvian taxes in honour of the English economist Arthur Pigou, who worked in this area), pollution permits, quotas, technology standards, and so on.

'Nature provides a free lunch, but only if we control our appetites.'
WILLIAM RUCKELSHAUS

> The true cost of all manufacture should also take into account the cost of any potential pollution – you pollute, you pay.

ADVERSE SELECTION

the 30-second theory

RELATED THEORY
See also
MORAL HAZARD
page 150

3-SECOND BIOGRAPHIES
GEORGE A. AKERLOF
1940–

JOSEPH E. STIGLITZ
1943–

MICHAEL SPENCE
1943–

30-SECOND TEXT
Aurélie Maréchal

3-SECOND CRASH
When buyers or sellers are missing information to make a good deal. Result? *Caveat emptor* (buyer beware) and *caveat venditor* (seller beware).

3-MINUTE BOOM
Information asymmetry is at the heart of the financial and banking sector. Stocks or currency transactions, credit and mortgage lending, all decisions are taken in uncertainty. Borrowers know more about their financial prospects, for example, than do lenders. Lenders respond (usually) with due diligence to confirm borrowers' creditworthiness. But there are limits. Toxic assets are a manifestation of adverse selection. The massive spread of these assets in the financial sector between 2007 and 2009 demonstrates the problems caused by information asymmetry.

When it comes to secondhand cars, nobody wants to buy a 'lemon', but it happens all the time. Why? Well, you may know that the average 10-year-old Ford trades for £5,000. The owner knows that, too. But he also knows whether his particular Ford is a gem or a clunker. If it's a gem, he might not be willing to sell at £5,000. But if it's a clunker, he'd be happy to let you have it. That gives you a big incentive to check the vehicle out; but the owner will still know more about it than you do. And that, in turn, may make you hesitant to cough up £5,000 for it. This example reveals that the market mechanism often doesn't function efficiently when one party has more information about the goods than the other – so-called 'information asymmetry'. Sellers may try to take advantage of this, trying to sell bad products that are overpriced. The same problem bedevils the market for health insurance, but the other way around. When insurers offer generous health insurance, they are more likely to attract unhealthy individuals with higher costs; this drives up the cost of insurance for everyone. To counter adverse selection, better information is needed for the party that is lacking it, for example, via a neutral intermediary (your local mechanic) or legal regulation (a compulsory medical checkup).

'For most cars traded will be the "lemons", and good cars may not be traded at all. The "bad" cars tend to drive out the good (in much the same way that bad money drives out the good).'
GEORGE A. AKELROF

> Does the nice salesman know something you don't? You'd better find out to avoid disappointment.

MORAL HAZARD

the 30-second theory

When an insurer sells vehicle insurance, he doesn't know the manner in which the vehicle is going to be driven, but he still has to set a price. The driver knows that the insurer lacks this information, so he's not worried about his premium rising if he drives dangerously, as long as he doesn't crash. On top of this, if he does crash, the damage will be paid by the insurer. This situation, when the owner has more information about how the vehicle is driven, and has less of an incentive to drive safely, is called 'moral hazard'. The owner's driving behaviour changes as a result of him having insurance, and this increases risk for the insurer. Even though the vehicle is owned by the driver, and he doesn't want it to be damaged, it is the insurer's responsibility if something goes wrong. Similarly, big companies or banks can be incentivized to take risks if they know they won't have to pay for any negative consequences of their actions. For example, if a company is treated as if it's 'too big to fail', and it believes the government will bail it out, it can make risky investments without worrying about the consequences.

RELATED THEORIES
See also
THE INVISIBLE HAND
page 136
ADVERSE SELECTION
page 148
GAME THEORY
page 108
RATIONAL CHOICE
page 106

3-SECOND BIOGRAPHY
KENNETH ARROW
1921–

30-SECOND TEXT
Aurélie Maréchal

3-SECOND CRASH
I am the one taking the risk, but someone else is responsible for it, and they'll pay if I fail.

3-MINUTE BOOM
The term 'moral hazard' is often taken to refer to fraudulent or immoral behaviour, but that doesn't have to be the case; moral hazard simply shows the challenges that markets may face in providing the best results for everyone. When information is not perfectly distributed, one party might be able to pursue its interest at the expense of the other. Of course, the other party has an incentive to design contracts that control this risk, and sometimes the intervention of the government may be necessary.

'Some particularly thorny issues are raised by the existence of financial institutions that may be perceived as "too big to fail", and the moral hazard issues that may arise when governments intervene in a financial crisis.'

BEN BERNANKE

> Only an individual really knows what he's going to do, but other people may have to pay to pick up the pieces if it all goes wrong.

EFFICIENT MARKET HYPOTHESIS

the 30-second theory

RELATED THEORIES
See also
FINANCIAL INSTABILITY
HYPOTHESIS
page 62
MORAL HAZARD
page 150

3-SECOND BIOGRAPHIES
EUGENE FAMA
1939–

MARTIN WOLF
1946–

30-SECOND TEXT
Christakis Georgiou

3-SECOND CRASH
Think you can outguess the stock market? That's a fool's errand, unless you know something the market doesn't.

3-MINUTE BOOM
The last 20 years, and especially the great financial crisis of 2007–2009, have created many problems for the efficient market hypothesis. Many prominent experts of financial markets, such as Martin Wolf of *The Financial Times*, now dismiss it as useless. The main attack against it is that it doesn't take account of psychological aspects of how finance works – what some dissident economists have called the 'herd instinct'.

These days finance seems to be the central issue in economics. But traditionally it was given attention once economists had developed theories to explain how the 'real' economy works. For a broad array of believers in the free market, financial markets function on the basis of the efficient market hypothesis. This is more or less an adaptation of general equilibrium theory. It assumes that in a financial market, such as Wall Street, the prices of traded assets – in this case stocks and bonds – already reflect all existing knowledge about them. Because of that, it is virtually impossible for any investor to consistently make gains by speculating on the prices of these assets. This is because until new information alters the value of an asset, no one can really know how its price will evolve. That means that only luck can help you when speculating, or indeed possession of insider information, which is forbidden by law. The efficient market hypothesis had circulated among economists for many decades before Eugene Fama at Chicago gave a standard version of it. It was the main theory for analyzing financial markets until the 1990s, when financial volatility and 'irrational exuberance' became the norm in finance.

'A market in which prices always "fully reflect" all available information is called "efficient".'

EUGENE FAMA

> If there's no new information about a certain stock or bond, you might as well roll dice to see if its price moves up or down.

RENT SEEKING

the 30-second theory

From large multinational firms to civil society groups representing the elderly, individuals and organizations lobby governments not simply in pursuit of the public good, but also to tilt the field in their favour. The aim of such behaviour is to capture 'rents' resulting from the price distortions and policy measures that come with government intervention. Valuable economic resources tend to be expended on the lobbying process, because competing special interest groups attempt to influence the content of policy. In response, bureaucrats do not act in the general public interest, but behave in the same self-interested manner as other economic actors and encourage 'rent seeking'. The result of this is the risk that the policies implemented in response to such lobbying will favour specific interests rather than serve the broader notion of the public good. It is those individuals and organizations that have more power in the political arena that benefit most from this process. The patterns of growth and distribution by which economic performance can improve are thus hindered by the artificial redistribution of resources through noneconomic means. Thus, in the aggregate, such a process of rent seeking reduces overall economic efficiency.

RELATED THEORIES
See also
CREATIVE DESTRUCTION
page 76
NEW TRADE THEORY
page 92

3-SECOND BIOGRAPHIES
GORDON TULLOCK
1922–

ANNE KRUEGER
1934–

30-SECOND TEXT
Adam Fishwick

3-SECOND CRASH
Economic performance suffers when narrow interests seek special political favours.

3-MINUTE BOOM
The concept of rent seeking is primarily used to highlight the negative impact of government policy. Yet the protections provided by such policy sometimes provide vital sources of economic growth. Copyright rules, for example, provide important protection for innovation that can be integral to rapid and sustained growth. And environmental regulations can provide real benefits, even as competing interests try to bend them to their favour. So can the benefits of government action outweigh the potential costs to efficiency?

'It is rational for individuals to invest resources to either increase the transfers that they will receive or prevent redistributions away from them. Thus, any transactions involving distribution will lead to directly opposing resource investments and so to conflict.'
GORDON TULLOCK

> *When special interest groups lobby government in order to affect policy in their favour, economic performance can suffer due to conflict.*

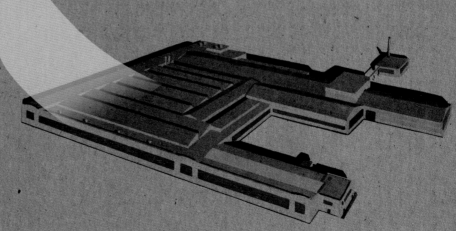

RESOURCES

BOOKS

The Economic Naturalist
Robert H. Frank
(Virgin Books, 2008)

Economics
Alain Alderton
(Causeway Press, 2006)

Economics
Paul Krugman & Robin Wells
(Worth Publishers, 2009)

The Economics of Global Turbulence
Robert Brenner
(Verso, 2009)

Economics Student Workbook
John Sloman & Peter Smith
(Financial Times Management, 2005)

Freakonomics
Steven D. Levitt & Stephen J. Dubner
(Harper Perennial, 2009)

Free to Choose
Milton & Rose Friedman
(Harvest Books, 1990)

The General Theory of Employment, Interest and Money
John Maynard Keynes
(CreateSpace, 2009)

Naked Economics
Charles Wheelan
(W. W. Norton & Co., 2003)

No Way to Run an Economy
Graham Turner
(Pluto Press, 2009)

The Return of Depression Economics
Paul Krugman
(W. W. Norton & Co., 2000)

The Undercover Economist
Tim Harford
(Random House, 2007)

The Wealth of Nations
Adam Smith; introduction by
Alan B. Krueger
(Bantam Classics, 2003)

The Worldly Philosophers
Robert L. Heilbroner
(New York Times Inc., 1961)

WEBSITES & BLOGS

The Conscience of a Liberal
krugman.blogs.nytimes.com
Economist and *New York Times*
columnist Paul Krugman's blog

EconLog
econlog.econlib.org
Daily blog from the Library of Economics
and Liberty – three bloggers write on
topical economics

Tim Harford's Financial Times columns
www.ft.com/comment/columnists/
timharford
Economist and journalist Tim Harford's
columns for *The Financial Times*

Greg Mankiw's Blog
gregmankiw.blogspot.com/2006/04/
time-inconsistency.html
Random observations for students
of economics – a helpful source for
explaining economic concepts

Marginal Revolution
www.marginalrevolution.com
Two economics professors, Tyler Cowen
and Alex Tababarrok, discuss the world
and news

Donald Marron
dmarron.com
Musings about economics, finance,
and life

New Economics Foundation
www.neweconomics.org
Professional resource for alternative
thinking on economics with analysis and
innovative propositions on current debates

Post-Autistic Economics Network
www.paecon.net
Database with free access to
hundreds of texts

Project Syndicate
www.project-syndicate.org/contributor/66
Harvard professor Dan Rodrik's column in
Project Syndicate

INDEX

ACKNOWLEDGMENTS

PICTURE CREDITS
The publisher would like to thank the following
individuals and organizations for their kind
permission to reproduce the images in this book.
Every effort has been made to acknowledge the
pictures, however, we apologize if there are any
unintentional omissions.

Alamy: 126 ©INTERFOTO

Corbis: 32 ©Roger Ressmeyer; 50 ©Hulton-Deutsch
Collection; 110 ©Ralf-Finn Hestoft

Getty Images: 18

Jupiter Images: 74, 94, 140